THE NEW SOLAR HOME

THE NEW
SOLAR

GIBBS SMITH
TO ENRICH AND INSPIRE HUMANKIND
Salt Lake City | Charleston | Santa Fe | Santa Barbara

HOME

DAVE BONTA & STEPHEN SNYDER

First Edition
13 12 11 10 09   5 4 3 2 1

Text © 2009 Dave Bonta and Stephen Snyder
Photographs © 2009 as noted on pages 150–51

Published by
Gibbs Smith
P.O. Box 667
Layton, Utah 84041

Orders: 1.800.835.4993
www.gibbs-smith.com
www.usasolarstore.com

Designed and produced by Debra McQuiston
Printed and bound in China
Gibbs Smith books are printed on either recycled, 100% post-consumer waste,
FSC-certified papers or on paper produced from a 100% certified sustainable
forest/controlled wood source.

Library of Congress Cataloging-in-Publication Data

Bonta, Dave.
  The new solar home / Dave Bonta and Stephen Snyder. — 1st ed.
     p. cm.
  ISBN-13: 978-1-4236-0390-0
  ISBN-10: 1-4236-0390-7
  1. Architecture, Domestic—United States. 2. Architecture and solar
radiation—United States. 3. Solar houses—United States. I. Snyder, Stephen,
1961– II. Title.
  NA7117.S65B66 2009
  728'.370472—dc22
                          2008053321

This book is dedicated to the memory of Dani Bonta's mother, Emilienne M. Clipet. She was a big part of our success story in Vermont and helped design our home as well as our guest cottage, which she dubbed Chaumiere d'Amis—the "Cottage of Friends."

We would also like to dedicate this book to the memory of Mitchell Smith, a visionary designer and creative green builder whose immense talents will be sorely missed.

cont

ents

acknowledgments

8

We cannot possibly express enough gratitude to the homeowners, architects, and builders who contributed to this book not only for their pioneering work in the sustainability movement but also in opening their homes to thousands of perfect strangers in hopes of making the world a better place. The generosity and enlightened worldview of these people taught us about so much more than just green homes: John Schaeffer and Nancy Hensley, Susan F. King and Harley Ellis Devereaux, Martha Matson and Cove Britton, Mitchell Smith, Steven Sheldon and IBIS, Angela Brooks and Lawrence Scarpa, Pugh+Scarpa Architects, Michael McDonald and Vince Wucherer, David and Lilliam Chengson, Betsy Armstrong and Richard Barr, Michael and Beth Yerke, David Dwyer, Michael and Joanne Frerking, Living Systems Sustainable Architecture, Karel and Alice Maritz Starek, Holly Aubry and LaForce+Stevens, J. Christopher Daly and the Sheldrake Organization, Ismael Leyva Architects, the Polshek Partnership, and David Rockwell.

Endless thanks to those unsung heroes who did whatever it took to pull countless elements together—usually at the last minute: Charity Grace Kirk at IBIS, Colin Gough at Gozzi Development, Daniel Safarik at Pugh+Scarpa, Daniel Alexander at Matson Britton, Jeff Davis, Rick Bascom, and Molly Gagnon at Davis Frame Company, and everyone at Gibbs Smith.

Many thanks to all of the helpful and talented photographers who truly made this book what it is not only through their art but also by helping us pull the project together in countless ways: Bruce Fiene, Barry Rustin, Barbara Bourne, Povy Kendal Atchison, Larry Kantor, Daniel Nadelbach, Marvin Rand, Wayne Capili and Interface Visual, Barnes Photographics, Sugar Pine Studios, and Steve Solinsky.

We also have to thank the world's best literary agent, Jeanne Fredericks, whose great interest in the subject matter of green living was such a huge help in finding homes and resources. Last, but not least, we want to thank our long-suffering families who endured the working weekends, shortened vacations, and all of the other demands of writing a book, especially Melissa, Virginia, and Ian Snyder.

introduction

I'd put my money on the sun and solar energy. What a source of power! I hope we don't have to wait until oil and coal run out before we tackle that."

—Thomas A. Edison, 1931

In our first book, *New Green Home Solutions*, we attempted to put in book form what we tell customers who come into one of our USA Solar Stores every day looking for information about renewable energy systems. We start with the basics of conservation and efficiency, follow up with an energy audit of their current home, discuss passive solar strategies, and then educate them about solar, wind, and micro-hydro systems and help them choose which suits them best. In this companion book, we have a different, although complementary, purpose. Here, we hope to dispel three main myths about renewable energy in general and solar homes in particular—that they are unattractive, overly expensive, and difficult places in which to live.

Although this book is primarily focused on passive and active solar homes, it is important to note that renewable energy is but one facet of a sustainable and healthy home. As one architect featured in this book put it, you can't just slap a solar panel on your house and call it green. Solar energy use must be paired with adopting an energy-conscious lifestyle, reducing your demand for electricity, using healthier and more earth-friendly building materials and household products, and conserving natural resources whenever possible.

We chose a variety of homes of varying sizes and locales to feature in the book, from 1,600 square feet to 4,000 square feet or more, and in large cities, suburbs, and remote rural sites. Many of them are the personal residences of renowned green architects or champions of green living—something we hope will give an insight into the best sustainable building practices from the leaders of this exciting movement. Others are homeowners who put their love of the planet and belief in environmental ideals to use in the place where we all spend most of our time—

our homes. All of them share a sense of responsibility to do their part to make the world a healthier place to live. No words on a page can quite capture the enthusiasm, optimism, and even the courage these pioneers expressed when relaying their commitment to renewable energy and green building, but we hope they will inspire you as much as they have inspired and taught us.

The homes in this book are meant to encourage, not intimidate. Clearly, these are exceptional homes that are groundbreaking not only in their use of renewable energy but also in their commitment to recycling and repurposing materials used in construction. These homes are focused on reducing the impact on the surrounding environment through sensitive building methods, as well as their use of nontoxic materials to create a healthier interior. However, all of the homeowners, architects, and builders stressed that each household should make personal decisions about what is affordable and sensible for them, and not feel that you have to be perfect or do everything all at once. Most of these

homes represent research, awareness, and practical knowledge that took years, if not decades, to develop. For most of them there were missteps, challenges, and false starts along the way—the price of taking risks and trying untested products and techniques. We hope this book will allow you to take advantage of their hard-won lessons and be the first of many steps toward your own green dream home. In the final analysis, we can do no better than to quote homeowner Dave Chengson, who is featured in the book and says, "I hope this book will contribute to the growing groundswell of people who are sensitive to energy resources, global warming, and the social impacts of oil, and serve as an inspiration for people to make a difference in their behavior, actions, and decisions." He also encourages people to lobby whomever they vote for so the political system will support and nurture a system that is more sustainable with our resources and planet.

DEFINING GREEN BUILDING

Not that long ago, green building simply meant energy-efficient building. Over time, though, the term has expanded its scope to include the use of sustainable materials and construction practices, healthy indoor environments, and techniques that account for the embodied energy of materials (including their transport), life-cycle costs of the building, and the ultimate recycling of used materials back into the building stream (green streaming).

solar basics

SOLAR HOT WATER

PASSIVE SOLAR

A passive solar home uses natural cooling and heating to condition the house without fossil fuels or energy-using mechanical devices. Passive solar heating systems capture solar energy within the building and slowly radiate that heat throughout the day as in this Davis Frame home in Vermont. The most basic passive-solar-heat techniques are referred to as direct gain and indirect gain. **+ Direct Gain**—With direct gain systems, solar energy enters the building through wide areas of south-facing glass, directly warming floors and walls. Warmth from the walls and floors is then radiated to the living area when

the inside air temperature falls below that of the heated mass. Clerestory windows and skylights are often used to boost the amount of sunlight striking the walls and floors. The amount of south-facing glass and thermal storage mass must be carefully designed because if the windows allow in more heat than the floor or walls can take up, overheating of the living space will result. Shading, overhangs, awnings, trellises, louvers, solar screens, and movable insulation are methods used to address this. With direct gain systems, the thermal storage mass can be less massive and more widely dispersed in the living area than with other passive-heating methods. This permits an even distribution of heat but requires careful consideration about how the living space is utilized.

Indirect Gain—Indirect gain passive design uses thermal mass or a sunspace to absorb solar heat and then transmit it to other areas in the evening and on cloudy days. Brick, masonry, concrete, and tile are examples of thermal mass that can absorb and then slowly release heat. In an indirect gain system, the thermal mass is located between the south-facing windows and the living space. Typical methods are an eight-to-twelve-inch-thick masonry trombe wall, or "water wall," of tubes or barrels placed behind the glass. During the day, solar energy passes through the windows and is collected in this thermal mass, which slowly releases its heat to the living space overnight. The delay as the mass warms and then releases heat keeps the temperature of the area fairly consistent. An added benefit is that the heating of the living space occurs later in the day, when it is most needed.

Materials with high thermal mass, which have the ability to absorb, store, and radiate heat, also work well in passive cooling. During the day, thick walls of concrete, adobe, or brick act as an energy-absorbing heat sink. When temperatures drop at night, the mass slowly releases the heat. For maximum effect, thermal mass must be exposed to the living spaces. High-mass buildings typically have as much as three square feet of exposed mass for each square foot of floor area.

Sunspaces—An attached sunspace, or "solarium," is typically constructed so it can be shut off from the rest of the home during times of severe heat and cold. Normally, the sunspace consists of a separate room on the southern wall of the home with extensive window glazing and some form of thermal storage mass. The sunspace may extend out from the house in a "solar bump" or the home can surround part of the sunspace, allowing less heat loss and more thermal mass to be placed inside.

Passive Cooling—Before air-conditioning, homes used natural ways of keeping cool in summer by breezes channeled through well-positioned windows, fountains in shaded courtyards, and with thick stone, brick, or mud walls to absorb the sun's heat. Today, these ancient methods as well as insulation, proper building orientation, and shading are used to passively cool sustainable homes. Passive cooling can, in fact, reduce or even eliminate the need for air-conditioning in many homes. Improving a roof's reflective quality can lower cooling costs by nearly half, depending on an attic's insulation. Experts advise installing highly reflective metal or tile roofing as well as putting a radiant barrier beneath the roof or in the attic floor. Dark roofs and walls retain 70 to 90 percent of the sun's radiant energy. Light-colored surfaces reflect solar energy and keep heat from being absorbed and transmitted from the attic to the living spaces below.

Natural Ventilation—Natural ventilation uses air movement to cool a home, often through open windows, skylights, and attic vents. Because moving air speeds evaporation on the body, a home's occupants can feel cooler at warmer temperatures if there is natural ventilation. Carefully placed openings on opposite sides of a home direct breezes through a house using cross-ventilation. Cross-ventilation can be improved with a thermal chimney, or thermosiphon, by operable windows and skylights at the lowest and the highest points in the structure. Ventilated attics are around thirty degrees Fahrenheit cooler than unventilated ones and solar-powered attic vents require no external power.

Evaporative Cooling—Evaporative cooling is used primarily in hot, dry climates like the southwestern United States. When water evaporates, the ambient air temperature decreases while relative humidity increases, making living spaces feel cooler. Foun-tains, pools, and transpiration from plants are all historical methods of using evaporative cooling to condition interior rooms. When that cooler air is directed through open windows or with fans, it can lower the temperature of interior living spaces. So-called "swamp coolers" are mechanical evaporative coolers often used in dry desert climates to condition the air.

Earth Berms—Constructing a home into a hillside is another very old technique for tempering the sun's heat and preventing heat loss in winter. Bermed, or earth-sheltered, structures take advantage of the cool, constant temperature of the earth since the ground is usually cooler than the air temperature in summer and warmer in winter. In hot climates, a mere twelve to twenty-four inches of soil built on a home's west-facing side can absorb heat and greatly lessen overheating.

ABOVE LEFT: These Davis Frame Company homes combine the classic feel of timber frame construction with a contemporary design that facilitates ample daylighting and passive solar heating.
ABOVE CENTER: Heat absorbing elements in this timber frame home, such as water or stone, collect the sun's energy during the day and slowly release it back into the living space at night. **ABOVE RIGHT:** A skillful balance of electric and natural light maximizes the comfort and functionality of living and work spaces.

Roof Overhangs—Properly designed roof overhangs are a passive solar architectural element positioned on the south-facing side of a house to block solar energy when the summer sun is high in the sky but to not obstruct the low-angled winter sun.

SOLAR HOT WATER

Photovoltaics, or solar electricity, are what most of us think of—and hear about—when renewable energy systems are discussed, but solar domestic hot water (SDHW) systems offer a less-expensive method of incorporating renewables into a home. In fact, a solar system that produces two-thirds of a home's domestic hot water can cost 90 percent less than a photovoltaic system. Plus, the payback on a solar water-heating system can range from five to ten years, faster than a photovoltaic system's estimated payback period. SDHW is a much more efficient use of the sun's energy at a lower cost; it is frequently used in radiant flooring for space heating but often works best as a supplement to standard and tankless on-demand water heaters in cold climates.

SOLAR HOT WATER COLLECTORS

Solar hot water collectors come in the form of flat plates that look similar to PV panels or as evacuated glass tubes. They can be installed anywhere the sun will strike them for four to six hours daily, but the roof is often the preferred spot. Green home builders often plan for the visual impact of solar collectors by designing roofs to hide them while siting the home for maximum solar exposure. As with PV panels, there has been a concerted effort made recently to lower their profile and make them less obtrusive on the home.

Solar hot-water systems will work with most conventional water heaters. Panels cost around $2,000 to $5,000 ($3,000 to $7,000 professionally installed) and typically reduce an average home's hot water bill by at least 60 percent—usually more.

SOLAR ELECTRICITY

Photovoltaic power captures the power of the sun to produce electricity and is dependable, generally maintenance free, and produces no greenhouse gases. Grid-connected solar electric systems provide quiet and trouble-free electricity. Systems with battery backup provide power during outages, and all of these systems can help you contribute to the fight against global climate change and increase your independence from expensive, vulnerable, and polluting sources of energy. Which system you choose will depend on a number of factors including your lifestyle, power needs, location, and budget.

Solar Module Life Spans

Solar modules are incredibly long lasting. The oldest home modules are still functioning perfectly after thirty years, as are most of the modules on satellites left in the harsh environment of space for decades. Nearly all solar-module manufacturers offer warranties of at least twenty years and, because they have no moving parts, PV modules are practically maintenance free.

Powering Appliances

Electric heat, refrigerators, and lights are the main 120-volt AC energy users in most homes, and these items should be upgraded with the most energy-efficient appliances available before buying a solar-power system. Essentially, any appliance powered by conventional utility power can be by run with solar. It should be noted, however, that 240-volt AC appliances drawing large energy loads, such as furnaces, air conditioners, water heaters, and stoves, are generally not practical to run with PV power since the system costs to create that much electrical power often outweighs the money saved by generating your own power.

YOUR SOLAR WINDOW

The time of day when the south face of your home is unshaded is called your "solar window" or "solar access zone." For active and passive solar methods to work successfully, this side of your home should remain in full sun at a minimum between 9:00 in the morning to 3:00 in the afternoon, solar time—where the sun is during standard, not Daylight Saving, time.

Water and Space Heating

Because most photovoltaic cells convert solar energy into electricity at such a low efficiency of around 15 percent, heating water and living spaces are not very practical uses of solar electric systems. Passive solar, the direct heating of air or water by the sun, is much more efficient for heating applications than PV.

Orienting Solar Modules

To properly install a PV system, it is essential to be aware of the placement and tilt requirements. PV modules must be aligned and angled to attain the greatest solar radiation and to avoid shading whenever possible. A PV module collects the most solar energy when it is at a ninety-degree angle to the sun. It should be angled to follow the sun's elevation during the course of the year and, if possible, turned to follow the sun's apparent path across the sky during the day. East-west tracking is possible with either an active or passive tracking system, which can boost your power potential by as much as 30 percent. However, because of the lower cost of today's PV modules with incentives, it is sometimes more cost effective to add more modules than to install expensive tracking systems.

"BALANCE OF SYSTEM" COMPONENTS

Solar-electric systems consist of several interconnected components to collect, store, and manage the power your home produces. One of the major strong points of these systems is their modularity. As your power needs evolve, components can be upgraded or added to boost capacity. Below is a brief summary of the equipment other than solar modules you will need in a typical solar-electric system.

Batteries—Several deep-cycle batteries are connected together in a battery bank, where they store the electricity generated by the solar array and release it as needed. (These are not used in grid-tie systems that forgo battery backup.)

Charge Controller—The charge controller keeps your batteries at a proper charge level and prevents them from overcharging.

Inverter—An inverter converts DC power generated by a solar array into AC power required to run most home systems and appliances.

Safety Fuses and Disconnects—These components consist of properly sized wires, fuses, combiner boxes, switches, circuit breakers, system monitors, and power meters that provide the proper safety features mandated for electric power systems.

Shading

Because most PV systems are wired together in a string like Christmas tree lights, shading of just one cell could reduce the power production of the entire module 75 percent or more. This is less of an issue with amorphous cells or modules wired in parallel. Likewise, solar hot water and solar hot air collectors are not as sensitive to shading, but as a general rule, all solar-energy systems should be installed to maximize solar access for as many hours as possible.

Grid-Tied Solar-Electric Systems

Grid-tied PV produces electricity and transmits it to the electric utility grid, offsetting your home's power usage and, in many cases, spinning the electric meter backwards. In many states, utilities offer credits to the homeowner for the electricity generated but not used. This credit is then used when the homeowner creates less power than is consumed. These agreements are called "net metering" or "net billing" and are one of the top benefits of using solar power.

Solar panels are used with dramatic and artistic effect on the Colorado Court apartment building in Santa Monica. Pugh Scarpa Kodama designed the forty-four-unit Colorado Court—the first Leadership in Energy and Environmental Design (LEED)–certified multifamily project. This LEED Gold building is also an affordable housing project that generates 90 percent of its own power.

Off-Grid PV Systems

Solar electric systems not connected to a utility are called "off-grid" or "stand-alone" systems. The two main types of stand-alone systems are direct systems (increasingly rare), which use the PV electricity as it is generated, and battery-backup systems (the most common form), which store solar-generated electricity for later use. While some off-grid homes use direct-current appliances, most off-grid systems with battery backup use an inverter to convert DC electricity from the solar array to alternating current so the more common AC appliances can be used.

SHOULD YOU WAIT FOR PRICES TO DROP BEFORE BUYING PV?

Many people who want to install a PV solar energy system often feel they should wait until the industry reaches economies of scale that will cause the prices to drop. Although there are continual breakthroughs in solar cell technologies that may lower costs significantly, it is debatable if this will happen in the short term. The demand and the price for the main component of solar panels, silicon, has skyrocketed in recent years—largely as a result of the stunning growth of the PV industry worldwide. Nevertheless, many architects, builders, and renewable-energy experts agree that recent advances in solar technology could overcome these issues and prices may drop dramatically in the next few years.

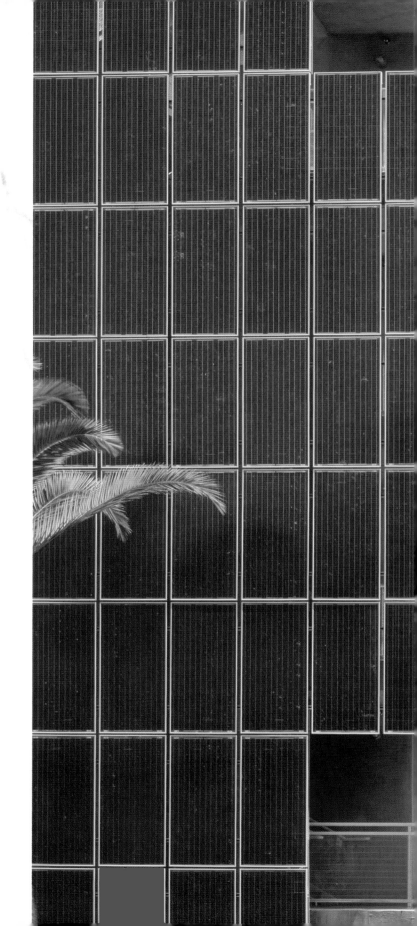

bonta home

WEATHERSFIELD, VERMONT

DESPITE THE CURRENT SPIKE in interest regarding all things green, especially green energy, a widespread misconception remains that emerged in the 1980s that "solar homes" are uncomfortable to live in, unattractive, and prohibitively expensive. Those homes that people are thinking of often had too much window glazing and were bristled with solar electric panels at odd angles, making them either too hot or too cold and frequently unattractive. Today's solar homes are quite different. Improved methods of passive solar heating and cooling as well as advanced technology have made those earlier homes a thing of the past.

My wife Dani Bonta and I also want to dispel the myth that solar homes are unaffordable by humbly offering our own house as an example. Because we did most of the site preparation and construction ourselves and carefully considered every choice we made from energy systems to appliances, our 1,600-square-foot off-grid home cost only $43 per square foot.

Despite common misconceptions about where solar power is effective, properly sited photovoltaic systems can work perfectly well on heavily wooded lots in northern climates like Vermont.

Our journey to living in a solar home grew from a desire to live in the country in the spirit of back-to-the-land pioneers Helen and Scott Nearing, who had headed into the countryside in the tradition of Thoreau. When building a new solar home, site selection is extremely important. While searching for property on which to build in Vermont, the first thing we looked for was land with lots of inherent natural resources—a south-facing slope, an earth berm against which to shelter the north side of the house, and lots of sheltering trees to the north. We also looked for wind potential in a northwest-facing exposure on a high elevation as well as lots of biomass

FACING: The open plan of the rustic cabin allows for easy heating by a centrally located woodstove as well as ample sunlight from south-facing windows.

ABOVE: A soapstone woodstove provides enough heat for the entire living space and uses only three cords of wood per year, which they cut themselves—so they have no heating bill. In addition, the south side of the house is warmed passively and filled with sunlight to lower electric lighting needs.

BELOW: The PV system uses 6 (42-watt) and 6 (64-watt) Uni-Solar amorphous panels wired in series to 24-volt and parallel as 3 strings of 2, which together lessen power loss when portions of the modules are shaded. **FACING ABOVE:** The north side of the home is bermed against winter wind and an unheated enclosed porch tightly sealed from the main house creates a dead air space to keep out the cold. The windows were recycled from a nearby demolition project. **FACING BELOW:** These Sunda evacuated solar hot water tubes are the first of their kind used in Vermont. They provide 60 percent of the home's domestic hot water and prefeed a radiant floor in the basement garage to keep the Bonta's biodiesel vehicles warm in winter for easy starting.

(trees) to burn and as possible construction materials. This site met all of our needs.

For us, solar electricity was a matter of necessity. There wasn't electricity on the property; to bring it in would have cost $24,000. Because of our attention to conservation and efficiency, our electricity needs are fairly light. A propane-powered generator provides extra power for loads not covered by the photovoltaic (PV) system.

The open plan of our rustic cabin allows for easy heating by a centrally located woodstove as well as ample sunlight from south-facing windows.

We wanted to build with local materials, so we bought a log home kit from a company in the area that uses environmentally friendly borate treatment on its

AN INSIDER'S VIEW

Dani Bonta advises, "Be energy conscious—change your lifestyle only in being more responsible with energy. Know what's turned on or off. And whether you start with a $3 lightbulb or a $5,000 hot water system, you can make the switch to sustainable living in increments. Not everybody should or even could be off-grid, but most homes can reduce a lot of the power they need and cut at least 50 percent off their utility bill."

The off-grid guest cottage, dubbed Chaumier d'Amis—the "Cottage of Friends"—by Dani's French-born mother, Emilienne, features a USA Solar Store micro solar power system, a composting toilet, pellet stove, and tankless water heater.

wood. We take the same approach with our food—eat locally, eat less, eat better. Although it's much easier to have a green home now than when we started our project in 1997, homeowners often must use what is available and what they can afford. There are other hard choices as well. Do you buy good products from countries with bad policies in hopes it will stimulate a more responsible economy there? In the end, everything has a balance that the homeowner must find. Our solar home provides freedom, beauty, and elegance without the normal economic constraints and the feeling that we are doing something that, taken together with the work of millions of others, can effect real change on the planet.

ENERGY-SAVINGS TIP: USE AN ENERGY MONITOR

Electric appliances can account for a sizable portion of your overall energy consumption and have a large impact on a renewable electricity system's size and cost. Energy monitors allow you to measure each appliance's energy use. Simply plug a Watts Up? Or Kill A Watt energy monitor into a wall socket and then plug the appliance into the device. It will reveal how much electricity each appliance uses.

ENERGY-SAVINGS TIP: GET AN ENERGY AUDIT

Professional energy auditors will help you identify the best ways to spend your energy dollars. You can find energy experts through your state energy office, the Residential Energy Services Network (http://www.natresnet.org), or the EPA's Home Performance with Energy Star program (http://www. energystar.gov/). An energy auditor uses infrared cameras to check for insulation deficiencies inside walls, and a blower door test to locate air leaks. Homeowners of a typical home can reduce their energy bills by one-third after conducting an energy audit and making the recommended changes.

In the kitchen, a super-efficient Conserv refrigerator-freezer consumes only 600 watts per day versus 1,600 to 2,000 for a conventional refrigerator, because it has no fans or heat tape for defrosting—a major power draw. Over the kitchen island, 7 watt mini CFLs (compact fluorescent lights) provide plenty of focused light close to the work area at a fraction of the cost of incandescent bulbs. All clocks are battery operated or wind-up.

vision,
post-and-beam,
to-live-in art

sunhawk home

HOPLAND, CALIFORNIA

NO TOUR OF BEAUTIFUL SOLAR HOMES, whether taken in person or in book form, would be complete without mentioning John Schaeffer, the founder and president of Real Goods, the nation's first and largest solar retail business and author of the indispensable guide to renewable energy products, *The Real Goods Solar Living Sourcebook*. In 1991, John created National Off-Grid Day, which evolved into the National Tour of Independent Homes the following year. Today, the National Solar Tour every October is the largest solar energy event in the world with more than 150,000 attendees visiting 5,000 buildings in nearly 3,000 communities.

SunHawk viewed from the South features a high tower for sweeping property views. The roof is covered with slate-like shingles made from 100% recycled rubber tires and gracefully incorporated solar modules. A sweeping front entrance accentuates SunHawk's curves and highlights an elegant redwood front door crafted from an old wine tank.

John and his wife Nancy Hensley believe a home is an expression of their values, and in 2001, this power couple folded all of their experience, principles, and knowledge of sustainability and off-the-grid living into a solar dream home in Hopland, California, ninety-five miles north of San Francisco. Just down the road is the twelve-acre Solar Living Center, headquarters of the nonprofit Solar Living Institute, which John chairs. A world-famous teaching center for green building, permaculture, and sustainable living technology, the center in many ways influenced the plans for John and Nancy's future home. Renowned green architect David Arkin of Arkin Tilt headed the project, which is so expertly oriented for maximum passive solar heating and daylighting that virtually no additional sources of light and heat are needed. Also, like the Solar Living Center, John and Nancy wanted a home with permaculture gardens, high thermal mass, and enough renewable-energy technology to supply all of their needs.

A friend recommended Berkeley architect Craig Henritzy, also a Native American cultural expert

GREAT GREEN FEATURES

- 4 kilowatts of Astropower 110-watt solar modules and 13 kilowatts of recycled Siemens 75-watt modules blown down by Hurricane Andrew
- Harris Hydroelectric Turbine producing 36 kilowatts per day from a seasonal creek
- House constructed primarily of Rastra Block (85 percent recycled Styrofoam, 15 percent cement)
- Recycled, reclaimed, or certified sustainably harvested wood used throughout the home
- Passive cooling and heating: southern orientation; super low emissivity windows; high thermal mass in slab and walls.
- Radiant floor slab heated by solar hot water panels and excess voltage from the hydroelectric system.

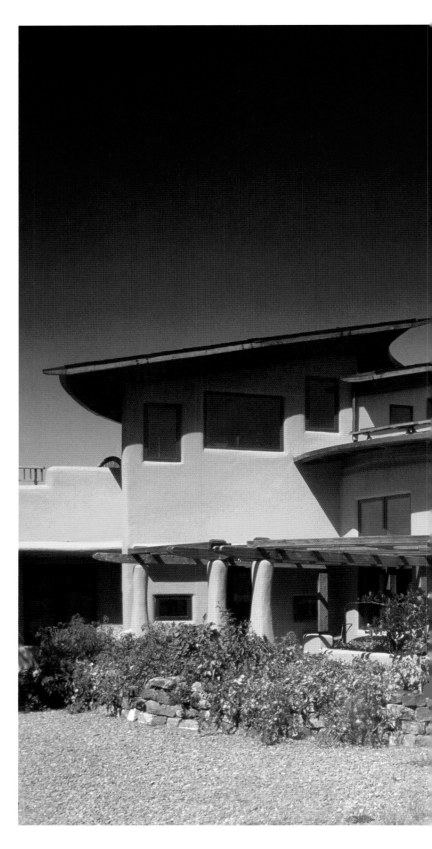

FACING: At SunHawk, the whole house acts as a solar calendar. In winter, the sun is lower, so it passes inside and strikes the Finnish soapstone fireplace opposite the front door at noon on the solstice. On the summer solstice, sunlight is directly on the front door and the stained-glass window above it. The inlaid hawk on the acid-stained concrete floor of the living room is illuminated by the sun precisely at solar noon on the equinoxes. In the tower, on the solstice and the equinox, the rays of the sun pass through various triangle-shaped notches at sunrise and sunset. ABOVE RIGHT: Recycled fir beams from a warehouse in Bayonne, New Jersey, greet the second floor balcony visitor. BELOW RIGHT: A glass block shower leads into a round bathroom filled with more recycled wonders.

and artist. Craig's expertise lies in applying ancient design principles to modern architecture and construction in a nature-sensitive way. Given John's role as a sustainable-living visionary and because hawks are often considered by native peoples as symbolizing vision, Henritzy designed a twenty-first-century version of a Native American roundhouse that resembles a hawk in flight. John had always wanted to live in a round home because of the sheltering feeling it provides; therefore, it was a perfect fit.

Historically, to have a passive solar house you had to have a rectangular structure with solar exposure on the long side. John and Nancy wanted the solar gain but didn't want a rectangular house, so the hawk shape Henritzy devised additionally worked perfectly for that reason. They got the round center they wanted, but the wings created a rectangle for the solar exposure. The resulting 2,900-square-foot home called SunHawk features hawk imagery throughout, including a tail-feather pattern in the beams and planks of the wood ceiling, wings that house the kitchen and a guest room, and a fanlike tail sheltering an outdoor terrace.

John and Nancy have always been intimately involved in the creation of their homes. When they bought their land in 1998, they camped around the property until they pinpointed the perfect spot for their green dream home. In 2002, they camped near a solar-powered barn on the property to watch the construction process unfold. John credits being so closely involved, as well as having solar power on-site from the very beginning, with making the whole homebuilding process cheaper and easier.

SunHawk's exterior walls are made of rastra blocks consisting of 85 percent recycled Styrofoam and 15 percent concrete-fly-ash mixture. Rastra block, which has an R-value of 35, was invented in Europe in the 1970s, using Styrofoam coffee cups and packing peanuts. It is fire- and termite-proof and the Styrofoam beads in rastra block make it easy to cut and sculpt, a major bonus when creating curved walls and fluid shapes.

An added green feature is that the home is virtually free of virgin materials and is a marvel of recycling and repurposing ingenuity. Granite countertops that look brand-new were repurposed from a Berkeley café that went out of business. Beams for the living room ceiling made their way to California from a naval warehouse in New Jersey that had collapsed. Rubber shingles with the look of slate but at half the price are made from recycled tires. The concrete is largely composed of fly ash, a by-product of coal-burning power plants. Redwood was recycled

from a winery. Walnut for flooring and cabinets was rescued from local land-clearing projects. Local craftsman Tom Boek made the willow furniture that graces the outdoor living spaces. Nancy did all of the research on recycled materials at salvage yards and recycling centers and spent countless hours on the Internet researching all kinds of found objects to repurpose. Allocate enough time for shopping around to find building supplies, Nancy says, and you can save two-thirds off conventional building products if you put enough time into finding the right materials. As a result of these and other wise conservation efforts, this eco-friendly dream home rich in character and artistry cost only about $195 per square foot.

In addition to the precise passive solar orientation, super low-emissivity (low-e) windows, and immense thermal mass, SunHawk also features a radiant floor slab with in-floor tubing to the first and second stories heated by solar hot water panels on the south-facing roof. A Finnish Tulikivi soapstone woodstove with a bake oven serves as the secondary heat source as well as a popular place for the family to make bread and pizza.

AN INSIDER'S VIEW

John's advice is well worth repeating: "Make sure your home is efficient first before going solar and insulate it as much as you can. Every dollar spent on energy conservation saves five dollars on energy generation." SunHawk is Nancy's fourth solar home, so her experience has taught her that deciding whether to start small or go all out on a solar home depends on your needs—who you are and where you are. She says that there is so much out there right now and so much more help at your fingertips than there used to be that it's easier to accomplish now what she and John did than it was even just a few years ago. Nevertheless, getting recycled wood is getting harder and more expensive she says, adding that home builders will need to come up with substitutions for wood materials. All of these will not be tried and true, she warns, so you have to be willing to pioneer if you want to do everything using alternative products.

A 10-acre pond provides passive cooling in the summer as well as inviting refreshing plunges on scorching 100+ Fahrenheit summer days. A "grotto" at the top of the pond provides respite from the summer heat and features exotic ferns as well as a handmade Mexican tin gorilla.

Although summer temperatures in Mendocino County regularly top one-hundred degrees Fahrenheit, the home stays cool without air-conditioning. Nine feet below SunHawk's core, an earth tube system with dual solar-powered fans draw sixty-seven-degree air from the ground up through two 150-foot culverts into the home. The home's innovative heating and cooling devised by their contractor, Steve Gresham, is very impressive, John says, but it works so well primarily because of Gresham's skillful overall passive heating and cooling design—the main reason SunHawk stays comfortable year round.

The home is set on 320 acres overlooking the Hopland Valley and is richly landscaped with gardens, orchards, and a lake with a waterfall that offers evaporative cooling to the home. A seasonal stream on the property feeds a 1,500-watt Harris micro-hydroelectric system that supplies thirty-six kilowatts of daily power from December through May. The hydropower system cost only $1,500 and, unlike wind or solar power, provides energy around the clock. Two ProgressiveTube fifty-gallon collectors on the roof use a five-watt PV (photovoltaic) panel for circulation. This type of self-contained solar water heater acts as a solar collector and storage tank in one unit. As a backup, their PV system not only provides seventeen kilowatts of electricity but also diverts any excess voltage to a heating element in their water tank. Another layer of redundancy lies in a propane backup system that can heat their water, if needed.

armstrong-barr home

SANTA FE, NEW MEXICO

BETSY ARMSTRONG AND RICHARD BARR say they were so grateful for having the means to build a green home that they sought to create a house that would minimize the demand on the world's dwindling resources. Living in the home with a young daughter, Richard and Betsy also wanted to make it as nontoxic as they could. Richard is a recently retired financial advisor who specialized in socially responsible investments. Coincidentally, Mitchell Smith, owner of Santa Fe's premier green-building firm, Solarsmith, was a longtime client and had discussed building a home for Richard and Betsy for years.

By first addressing issues of energy, water, and material with Smith, Betsy and Richard came up with a design that would reduce the home's ecological footprint to an extent far smaller than its outward appearance would suggest. The home was finally completed in 2003 after six months of planning and then a full year searching for the right piece of land, but it was well worth the wait. Perched on a narrow ridge in the Santa Fe foothills, the home offers sweeping views of the Jemez and Sangre de Cristo mountains out the living room window, and the Sandia Mountains from the portal (pronounced "poor-tall," a southwestern architectural term for

a covered patio or entry). Richard and Betsy bought land in a high-end neighborhood but did not want a high-end house. The Solarsmith home is designed in the pueblo style of architecture, which is adobe with curved walls and buttresses. Smaller than nearby homes, the living area is 3,000 square feet with an additional 500 square feet devoted to a 2,500-gallon solar-heated exercise pool.

Mitchell Smith used "thermal envelope" construction of exterior walls that are double framed with a two-inch layer of closed-cell insulation foam outside, which repels heat and cold while maintaining a comfortable temperature inside. Smith also

Several rooms open to the lawn and gardens, creating a direct connection
to the outside as well as aiding natural cooling.

positioned the home to take advantage of passive solar heating. The house faces south to capture winter sun, and a sheltered western side protects it from New Mexico's intense summer sun, so much so that the home does not require mechanical air-conditioning.

Clerestory windows sixteen feet above the kitchen floor bring daylight into the home's core and double as passive-cooling vents. The homeowners open the windows in the spring and close them in late autumn. Between April and November, a gentle convective current allows warm air to escape while drawing in cooler breezes from below. Lighting comes from

AN INSIDER'S VIEW

There were no solar tax credits in New Mexico when the Armstrong-Barrs built their home, so they missed out on $10,000 that they would have received with the state's current incentives. Richard and Betsy's advice is familiar among green homeowners: get involved in the design and construction or you have yourself to blame for any disappointments. Know what you want and have a close relationship with the designer and builder; if you can find one person who can be both the designer and builder, it will be a big asset. They credit their designer/builder, Mitchell Smith, with support of, expertise in, and sensitivity to their goals in making their home such a successful example of sustainable living.

LEFT: The 200-square-foot portal holds an outdoor bed and furniture and opens onto a lawn irrigated by rainwater runoff from the roof.

a combination of energy-efficient compact fluorescents and low-voltage lights. The house itself is an R-57 super-insulated building envelope. General orientation contributes to passive solar heating and cooling along with their passive solar greenhouse. Most of the year Richard and Betsy's electric bill is around $30 per month for their 3,500-square-foot home. In severe winters, when Santa Fe typically

GREAT GREEN FEATURES

- Super-insulated building envelope with an average rating of R-57
- No-VOC natural gypsum plaster walls
- Grid-tied photovoltaic system
- Low-voltage lighting and CFLs (compact fluorescent lights)
- Passive cooling and heating; no mechanical air-conditioning
- Sustainably harvested and FSC-certified woods throughout
- Ten-thousand-gallon cistern to collect rainwater runoff for landscaping
- Waste-digester system to irrigate the lawn and orchard

The poolroom, featuring banana trees, also doubles as a greenhouse.

receives thirty-five inches of snow, the cost of heating is about half of what their neighbors pay.

Whenever possible, sustainable forest products were used throughout the home and local craftspeople were employed. The flooring is FSC (Forest Stewardship Council)-certified cherry wood from Vermont. The vigas and framing lumber came from a local supplier employing sustainable management and was harvested from dead-standing spruce. Windows, doors, and cabinet wood also came from sustainably managed forests. The entire house is clad with oriented strand board made from trees reclaimed from a forest fire site and a tree-thinning project. The plank decking in the ceiling and the beams came from a local supplier who selectively thinned his ponderosa pines for fire protection. The structural beams are glulam, a manufactured product that replaces the use of old-growth beams. The roof deck is a Trex deck made from recycled plastic and wood fibers. Natural gypsum plaster was used on interior walls to minimize VOCs (volatile organic compounds) and chemicals, and, where possible, ABS (Acrylonitrile-Butadiene-Styrene) plumbing pipe was used as a greener alternative to PVC (polyvinyl chloride).

The exterior of the house makes skillful use of xeriscaping with drought-tolerant low-maintenance native plants that blend wonderfully into the arid Santa Fe landscape; this is perfect for the owners because they are often out of town and are not home to water. A rooftop rainwater-collection system with a 10,000-gallon storage cistern supplies most of their landscaping needs. A Pumice Wick human waste digester and waste-water nutrient supplier supplements the cistern by utilizing gray and black water from the home. All appliances are water- and energy-efficient.

For all of the great green features, what Betsy and Richard love most about their home is what cannot be seen. On the roof, a 2.8-kilowatt grid-tied photovoltaic system and two solar hot-water collector panels supplement much of their electric and domestic hot-water needs. And the Armstrong-Barrs share their eco-friendly housing success with the neighbors; their grid-tied solar system not only helps heat water for the radiant floors, exercise pool, and appliances, but it also feeds surplus energy to

TUBULAR SKYLIGHTS

Tubular skylights are composed of a clear acrylic dome on the roof that captures sunlight, a highly polished reflective steel or aluminum pipe that carries light through the attic, and a flush or domed fixture in the ceiling that diffuses light throughout the room. Tubular skylights are easy to install, bring natural light to rooms too small for a full-sized skylight, and can be installed for less than $1,000.

ENERGY-SAVINGS TIP: BUY POWER STRIPS

A so-called "phantom load" is the small amount of electricity used when devices appear to be turned off. The main culprits are plug-in power adapters and appliances with digital clocks, indicator lights, remote controls, or instant-on functions. While a couple of watts of standby energy use per appliance may seem trivial, phantom loads in a normal home employ more than one kilowatt-hour daily. By using timers or power strips to control these loads, you will not only limit your energy usage but will also reduce the size of a planned renewable-energy system. Televisions, DVD players, and office equipment are examples of appliances that, when put on a power strip, can easily be turned off when not in use. Just make your power strips visible and accessible so you will actually use them.

Solar panels and a Trex deck
made of recycled plastic.

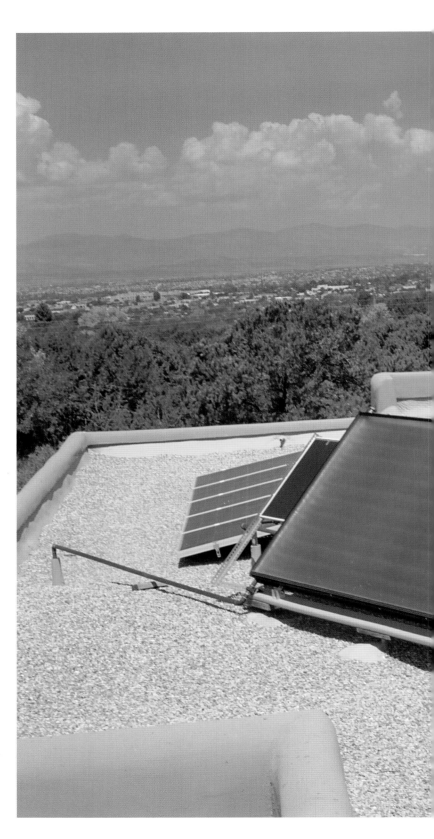

neighboring homes. In line with their desire to give
something back to the community, the 140-watt
rooftop solar panels generate the home's electricity and any extra is fed to the neighborhood, using
a system that locates the nearest energy need and
sends power to that home.

Richard and Betsy say that it is also important
to have a good plumber and electrician put in solar
energy systems because they are still fairly unique
and the average trades person may not have the
ability to install them properly. Richard estimates a
payoff period of eight to twelve years, depending on
what you spend on your solar energy system and the
price of electricity. Nevertheless, he counsels that if
you have the resources, try to look past the money
because it is the right thing to do. If money is a problem, simply look at what you *can* do. Maybe add a few
solar panels or rain barrels to conserve water, but,
above all, super-insulate your house.

GRAY WATER

Household wastewater is called gray water, except for water
from toilets (which is called black water). Dishwasher, sink,
bath, and laundry water comprise 50 to 80 percent of residential wastewater and are a valuable resource that can be reused
for landscape irrigation and other purposes. Recent concerns
over declining water resources and overburdened sewage
treatment plants have elevated interest in recycling gray water. Currently, only New Mexico, California, Utah, and a few
other states allow underground drip gray-water irrigation.

A few of the benefits of using gray water are the following:
• Reducing fresh water usage
• Less strain on failing septic tank or treatment plant
• Less energy and chemical use
• Boosting groundwater
• Recovery of wasted nutrients

cutting edge,
titanium roof
natural beauty...

gozzi home
CARMEL, CALIFORNIA

DANIELE GOZZI VISITED the United States in the 1980s and fell in love—especially with California and the Monterey Peninsula. In 1989, he and his wife Anita bought land there. In 1994, he decided to leave his European architectural office and start from scratch in America. Today, he is CEO of Gozzi Development, Inc., and Anita, an MBA, serves as president of the company. Daniele's years of experience have provided him with an extensive network of suppliers and manufacturers throughout Europe. In addition to architecture, Daniele produces custom designs in clothing, furniture, kitchens, dental cabinetry, and interior décor. Their other company, Mobili, Inc., was founded in 1994 as a premier importer and distributor of contemporary European office and residential furniture.

Perched high above the family room, the formal dining area boasts a panoramic view of the Pacific Ocean and surrounding hillsides. The large round dining table and the accompanying "Ingram High" chairs were designed by C.R. Mackintosh. Hand made of ash wood in Italy, the table comfortably seats eight for a sunset dinner.

Born and raised in Switzerland, Gozzi has more than thirty years of experience in the architectural, design, and construction fields dating back to an architecture apprenticeship at the age of sixteen. Although Daniele's current personal tastes are for the ultra contemporary, in Europe he specialized in renovating medieval buildings, which developed in him a deep appreciation for the values of old-world craftsmanship. Gozzi notes that Europe has embraced for many years the green-building practices of conservation and using eco-friendly products. He brought these principles with him to the United States in 1994 as a standard way of doing business.

AN INSIDER'S VIEW

Daniele Gozzi has seen some changes in green-building attitudes over the past few years, but still, few builders seem eager to try new methods and products, which he attributes to the profit motive winning out over benefits to the homeowners in many cases. He says that a good designer and builder will not focus just on maximizing profit. Nevertheless, he does see a more green future on the horizon—with more clients being open to a greater use of insulation and concrete, and to building with recycled materials. He also thinks improvements in solar power will drop prices dramatically. His advice: "Start now and put in insulation, renewable-energy systems, recycled products; use nonpolluting technology; and install conduits for updating and expanding your renewable energy systems. Great planning saves a lot of money and material. Don't focus on the pennies. It is not just about what the bank account says but about investing in your kids' future now. Ultimately, use common sense and your own hands to conserve energy, especially when it comes to turning off lights and appliances."

the home is constructed almost entirely from concrete, using Greenblocks, an environmentally friendly product from Switzerland

An expert in energy efficiency, Gozzi is captivated by what he calls "smart home" technologies. He admits that he is always looking for new ways to make home systems greener, whether he is doing a remodel or a completely new home-building project. Daniele credits Anita's great intuition with new technology, as well as her level-headed business instincts, with controlling his desire to experiment with every green product he finds. Because Daniele has an enormous appetite for knowledge of new products, he insists on testing products in his own home before using them in client projects. He says he is happy to be the guinea pig. Many times he is fortunate he did prior testing when prototypes used in the home did not work as planned. As a result, he says most of their clients come from referrals and remain lifelong friends.

Although the permitting process took years, he built his 8,000-square-foot home in just ten months. The home is constructed almost entirely from concrete, using Greenblocks, an environmentally friendly product Gozzi brought in from Switzerland for projects in Southern California in the late 1980s. The highly polished floors are concrete as well with Versace Porcelain tiles on top. With longstanding business relationships as well as offices in Switzerland, Germany, and Italy, Gozzi buys materials

FACING: The suspended dining area features custom stainless steel railings with clear acrylic panels and a spiral stairway to the lower level. **ABOVE LEFT:** A clean, ultramodern European sensibility influences the Gozzi home. **ABOVE RIGHT:** Just south of Pebble Beach and sitting on over two acres, the Gozzi home overlooks the Pacific Ocean and borders land owned by the California Coastal Conservancy.

GREAT GREEN FEATURES

- Super-insulated titanium-zinc alloy roof has an R-50 value
- Ten-kilowatt-per-hour PV system, geothermal heat pump, and solar hot water systems provide all heat and hot water
- Low-e windows imported from Switzerland are even more energy efficient than models available on the American market
- Greenblock recycled polystyrene building forms are used in all the interior and exterior walls
- All outdoor lights are solar powered; inside they use CFLs and LEDs exclusively
- A home-automation system helps keep unused lights off and controls energy usage

The kitchen super-efficient appliances include a SubZero Refrigeration system along with a Meile cooktop, dishwasher, oven and steamer.

directly, shipping them to the United States. As a result, his own home is filled with some of Europe's best cutting-edge products—from super-energy-efficient doors and windows; lighting imported from Switzerland; stainless-steel railings, titanium roof, and cabinetry from Germany; and Italian tiles, a glass mosaic, and furniture. When he built his family's home on the South Coast on Highway 1, he tested state-of-the-art geothermal and passive solar techniques, and photovoltaics, as well as eco-friendly materials and construction methods. The result, he says, is that although they have radiant in-floor heating, it never has to be used.

Among Gozzi's greatest finds are the low-e Swiss windows in the house that open to the inside, but also tilt open to allow in fresh air, and when closed allow enough sun to warm the house to a year-round seventy-five degrees Fahrenheit. The home also features a super-insulated titanium-zinc alloy roof to resist the corrosive effect of the coastal atmosphere. Used for years in Europe, the metal standing-seam

INSULATED CONCRETE FORMS

Insulated concrete forms (ICFs) are hollow polystyrene blocks stacked as the exterior walls of a house, reinforced with steel rebar and then filled with concrete. This wall system supplies outstanding strength, energy efficiency, and sound dampening. Greenblock ICF walls provide a consistent R-39 thermal resistance over the life of the product. Coupled with the thermal mass qualities of concrete, as well as the absence of air, a Greenblock 10-inch ICF provides a wall system comparable to an R-50 wood-framed wall, and cold spots are reduced by eliminating the thermal bridging of wood-frame construction. ICFs are also up to 70 percent less expensive to heat and 50 percent less expensive to cool than traditional wood-frame construction.

The Gozzi's solar heated indoor pool is completely covered by Bisazza Italian imported glass mosaic.

roof also made it easy to attach racks for their photovoltaic and solar hot water systems. The ten-kilowatt-per-hour photovoltaic (PV) system on the garage roof provides all of their electricity, while a geothermal heat pump and solar hot water unit heat the home and keep the indoor pool a steady ninety degrees Fahrenheit.

In the kitchen, all appliances are the most energy efficient he could find. The Miele dishwasher, for example, senses when there is not a full load and adjusts accordingly. All of the home's outdoor lights are solar powered, while inside they use CFLs and cutting-edge LEDs (light-emitting diodes). A sophisticated home-automation system (controllable over the Internet when the Gozzis are away from home) helps keep unused lights turned off and manages household energy usage.

Long committed to the highest level of environmental responsibility, Daniele says it is wonderful to see so many more homeowners in America embrace green principles, especially in his part of California. He attributes the natural beauty of the area with inspiring the strong dedication to preserve it.

ARE BIG HOMES GREEN?

There is a movement advocating a return to smaller homes because larger homes waste resources. However, the cost per square foot is often higher for a small home than that of a larger home. When building a larger home, the expense of the most costly items that every home must have (such as a furnace or kitchen) is spread over more square footage. As a result, a larger home may have a lower square-footage cost than a smaller home. Also, it usually costs less to build a two-story home when compared to a one-story home that has the same square footage. This is because a two-story home will have a smaller roof and foundation, and plumbing and ventilation systems are more compact in two-story homes.

reclaimed woods,
post-and-beam,
to live in art

starek home
BOULDER, COLORADO

EVOKING THE CHAMBERED-NAUTILUS shape of the universe seen in countless designs of nature, the Starek home seems part fairy-tale castle and part M. C. Escher sketch. Clearly, the home of Karel and Alice Maritz Starek defies the conventions of what one thinks of when conjuring up images of a solar home. This lyrically crafted jewel in Boulder, Colorado, contains all of the best elements of a sustainable home—renewable energy, high thermal mass, recycled and reclaimed woods, natural plasters, stone, and adobe, as well as nontoxic finishes and paints. Even better, Karel and Alice called upon a veritable army of local artisans and craftspeople to make this fantasy home a reality.

RIGHT: A secluded Jacuzzi well hidden from view overlooks the majestic scenery outside Boulder.
FACING: Despite all of the home's interesting features that make everybody want to get inside and see the house, the landscape is the most popular with guests because it ties nature to the house so well, with layers of space that are partially indoors and partially outdoors.

AN INSIDER'S VIEW

The owners believe that homebuilding in America has become so focused on size and money; i.e., the biggest house for the least money possible. The Stareks focused instead on a reasonably sized house for their budget. Alice says they were not stressed about their budget because it was kept low enough to allow for wiggle room, which gave them a nonadversarial relationship with the builders and a lack of typical financial-based fear. She philosophically describes the building process as a partnership where what you put in is what you get out. "If love, friendship, loyalty, and teamwork go into a house, then you're going to have a much more rewarding place to live in, and you will feel better about the home in the end. If you pay a worker a reasonable rate and treat them well, it's amazing what comes back to you," Alice says. Another problem she sees is that houses are often built to eliminate a connection to nature; e.g., a garage connected to a house to avoid the elements, but as a result exhaust from the car ends up in the living room. People often want to build a home to meet every possible need, such as designing the house to perfectly accommodate a party for 120 people and a live band. Resist that temptation (and others) and you will save a lot of square footage. Not only will this save you money, but it will cause you less stress as well, she counsels. A well-designed smaller home will have a wonderful feel, create more intimacy in your life, meet your real needs, be simpler and less expensive to maintain, and enhance your lifestyle.

The construction itself took six years amid the demands of family, work, and the ebb and flow of building budgets and the seasonal nature of doing construction high in the Rockies. The genesis of their home actually began years earlier, when, as a graduate student, Alice (now principal architect with Alma Designs) was studying architecture at Washington University. A visiting professor asked her students to design a house following the mathematical shape and form of a piece of music. She recommended Beethoven's 3rd for Alice's project. The end result showed up years later in their present adobe and stone home.

How things tie together has always been important to Alice, and she believes in connecting with the planet and the life around her. Alice's belief is that beyond the basic human needs, you need to meet the needs of your soul. "Dig into that, live that, find beauty in that," she says. For her, living green is not because it is the right thing to do or a feeling of guilt about resources she's wasting, but about finding herself. Happiness and connection to the world around her are driving forces in her life, so using solar is a natural spin-off of that lifelong search for our place in the natural world.

"All of us need a connection to the earth," Alice says, and, as an architect, she enjoys helping people find their connection. The Starek family does not seek a steady-state comfort level. Sometimes comfort is a

BELOW: Plants, original artwork and a handcrafted stone fireplace lend a connection to the natural world that the Starek's treasure. FACING ABOVE: The dining room sits in an attached greenhouse, where the Stareks grow herbs, citrus fruits, and flowering tropical plants. FACING BELOW: The upstairs floors in the Starek home are covered with sound-absorbing sustainable cork.

every home you live in, changes your mindset in very subtle and hard-to-measure ways. It's like when you listen to a piece of music that makes you sad, mellow, or contemplative. A home is the same way, and that's why design and material selection is so important, Alice says. She freely admits that their home is not as simple as most homes. It is complicated, with active and passive solar features; these features cost more, which is a negative, but as an artist, she feels a need to express herself through art and to live in art.

The Stareks were intimately involved in building the house and didn't hire a contractor per se but instead used a team of artisan craftspeople and friends. This makes having a set budget next to impossible; however, it can deeply enrich the experience of building a home as well as help form meaningful relationships that can last a lifetime. As an architect, Alice says she spends just as much time counseling people as she does designing because couples looking for different things often have trouble reconciling their desires when so much money is involved. Not surprisingly, she often catches herself lecturing her clients over lifestyle choices.

distraction from meaning, and having a house a perfect sixty-eight or seventy-two degrees Fahrenheit every day of the year doesn't work for her. She likes the connection to the seasons—being a little colder in winter, warmer in summer. Needing to light a fire in the fireplace for comfort adds to one's life experience, she says.

Connection with the earth is a big part of this house. The first-story floors are all adobe crafted with dirt from outside the home with water and gravel the family mixed themselves. Linseed oil was used to finish and harden it. Alice likes the fact that with adobe there is no insulation, concrete, or steel separating them from the energy of the earth. She astutely observes that every building you walk into,

ENERGY-CONSCIOUS
LIFESTYLE TIP: USE DAYLIGHT

For free illumination during the day in dimly lit spaces, install solar light tubes, a recent innovation that brings sunlight into a home through a series of mirrors and highly reflective surfaces. Skylights can work as well but can let in excessive heat in the summer and draw out precious heat on cold days if they do not have proper glazing.

BELOW: The kitchen, located at the center of the first floor of the house, gets most of its light from the adjacent greenhouse. FACING: Reclaimed wood shows up in the ceiling beams and furniture, including cabinets, bed platforms, and shelves.

GREAT GREEN FEATURES

- Thermal coupling-high thermal mass
- Solar electric system
- Solar hot water system
- Local stone, natural plaster, and adobe used throughout
- Cork flooring with a water-based sealant
- Locally milled and reclaimed wood
- Energy-efficient Cempo building forms made from recycled polystyrene
- Super-efficient appliances and no clothes dryer. (All laundry is hung outdoors in summer and indoors in winter to humidify the air.)

Every decision has to be carefully considered when not using standard products, Alice says. In Boulder, they found it easy to locate green products, but some builders are not aware of eco-products and you have to do your own homework. Details are important too. Adding CFLs is good, but where you place them is also crucial. If the CFLs are up in the ceiling or too far away from the countertop where you need them, it's terribly inefficient. Nevertheless, Alice notes there is no such thing as a perfect design.

The adobe blocks used in the home were leftover from other construction jobs. The walls are constructed from Cempo Forms, a building system made of Portland cement and recycled polystyrene. The name *Cempo* is an acronym for "cement polystyrene" and features a series of channels running horizontally and vertically through the forms. The channels are filled with structural concrete and rebar, effectively creating a post-and-beam matrix inside a "sandwich" of the composite. Besides being energy efficient, these panels divert tons of bulky, nonbiodegradable polystyrene from landfills.

A 4.14 kilowatt solar energy system provides most of the electricity for the home while the home's heating, hot water, and hot tub are all provided by the solar hot water system. The Stareks are exploring wind power as an option to provide the balance of their electrical needs.

ENERGY STAR HOME RATINGS

To earn the Energy Star, a home must meet strict guidelines for energy efficiency set by the U.S. Environmental Protection Agency. These homes are at least 15 percent more energy efficient than homes built to the 2004 International Residential Code, and include additional energy-saving features that typically make them 20 to 30 percent more efficient than standard homes. Energy Star–qualified homes can include a variety of the following conventional energy-efficient features that contribute to improved home quality, homeowner comfort, lower energy demand, and reduced air pollution:

- Effective insulation
- High-performance windows
- Tight construction and ducts
- Efficient heating and cooling equipment
- Efficient products
- Third-party inspection to verify the energy efficiency measures as well as insulation, air tightness, and duct-sealing details.

yerke home

CHICAGO, ILLINOIS

MICHAEL AND BETH YERKE owned a home on Chicago's north side that needed some serious work. So much so that they decided it would make more economic sense to knock it down and build new. They engaged a local architect whose designs they liked and began looking for a contractor. That's when Beth's mother suggested green builder Dave Dwyer. A friend who is a builder advised them to go with a person they could have a good relationship with if the project estimates were similar, because the choice of builder can determine whether the homebuilding process was a nightmare or a rewarding learning experience. They met Dave, immediately liked him, and decided to hire him for the job.

Gas fireplaces help take the chill out of Midwest winters. The Yerkes offset their negligible natural gas and electricity use with carbon-emission offsets and renewable-energy credits.

IEQ IQ

Indoor Environmental Quality (IEQ) refers to the quality of the air and environment inside buildings, based on pollutant concentrations and conditions that can impact the health, comfort, and performance of occupants—including temperature, relative humidity, light, sound, and other factors. Good-quality IEQ is an essential component of any building, especially a green building. According to the EPA, in recent years, scientific evidence has indicated that the air in our homes can be more polluted than the outdoor air in the nation's major cities. Even worse, studies indicate that most people spend approximately 90 percent of their time indoors (source: EPA).

Michael says they did not go into the project intending to build a green home until Dave started talking to them about the possibilities in detail. He compared the expense of an HVAC system to the costs of a green-energy system, which showed the Yerkes that the yearly operating cost of the renewable system would be at least $5,000 less than a conventional one. The Yerkes quickly knew this was how they wanted to proceed. Dave tweaked the original Patricia Craig design, making the formal dining room smaller and the family room larger for a more realistic accommodation to the family's lifestyle. Dwyer also made the master bedroom and bathroom slightly larger.

The key green features Dwyer brought to the 4,350-square-foot brick home completed in 2005 are its solar hot water and geothermal systems. The geothermal unit, in conjunction with the solar thermal system, supplies the Yerkes with hot water, radiant in-floor heating, forced-air space heating, and

GEOTHERMAL HEAT PUMPS: THE BEST-KEPT SECRET IN RENEWABLE ENERGY?

Although geothermal heat pumps have been around for many years, the rising cost of home heating and concerns over climate change have increased interest. Geothermal or ground-source heat pumps basically tap into the earth, where the temperature stays relatively constant between fifty and fifty-five degrees Fahrenheit regardless of the outside temperature. Geothermal heat pumps circulate a food-grade glycol-antifreeze mixture through pipes buried deep in the ground, drawing heat from the earth in winter and transferring it back into the ground in summer. These systems use a fraction of the electricity of conventional HVAC systems and, according to the EPA, can cut cooling costs by 50 percent and heating costs by as much as 70 percent. The downside is the expense. Digging the wells alone can cost thousands of dollars and entire systems generally run $30,000 to $40,000. The good news is that government incentives are available to lower the upfront costs, and new technologies are rapidly appearing that may cut the price dramatically in the next few years.

even air-conditioning. Dwyer also employed energy-efficient strategies to create a home meeting Energy Star standards and having virtually no carbon dioxide emissions.

Although the home and its systems are pioneering, Michael Yerke says they have not required any lifestyle change for the family. In addition, because the renewable-energy systems are hidden on the roof and buried underground, if you didn't tell them, no one would know they were there. Nonetheless, neighbors and friends are very inquisitive about their system (which cost around $18,000 after state and federal incentives and rebates), and the Yerkes are more than happy to tell them of the system's expected five- to six-year payoff. While Michael says he can only guess at the savings compared to neighbors because so many lifestyle factors come into play— number of people at home all day, number of children, and so on—they are saving approximately $300 per month.

"People should definitely go this route," Michael insists, saying that energy prices will only go up and homeowners who invest in these systems will get their money back over time. In the meantime, it makes you feel a lot better that you are saving money and doing less damage to the environment. The Yerkes say they were happy to make a greater front-end investment for this system. They have a daughter now and want to lead by example.

Dave Dwyer, LEED accredited since 2004 and an Energy Innovator Award winner, has since decided to focus on renewable energy rather than green building. Dwyer says that 20 percent of the embodied energy in a building's life cycle is used toward erecting a building, while 80 percent is in the operation of that building over its lifetime. Therefore, he decided he would have more of a positive environmental effect if he shifted his focus to the 80 percent. As a result, the Yerke's Lincoln Park home was his last building project. Like the Yerkes, Dave and wife and partner Dr. Toni Bark felt they had to do something worthwhile beyond their previous experience and wanted to do something their kids would be proud of. Through their company, American Renewable Energy, Dwyer

Large doors to a multi-level deck invite natural cooling and ample daylighting. Furniture made from recycled and organic materials and sustainably harvested wood floors give the inviting eco-friendly family room warmth and texture.

GREAT GREEN FEATURES

- Solar thermal system creates hot water and radiant heat
- Geothermal heating and air cooling cut costs
- Renewable-energy credits purchase electricity from wind farms
- Carbon credits offset the natural gas used by the stove and fireplaces
- Floors and staircases are Forest Stewardship Council–certified Brazilian cherry with all-natural resin finishes
- Locally crafted furniture is made with organic wool batting, natural latex foam rubber, and wood from salvaged trees
- Energy Star–qualified windows provide better insulation

now designs, builds, and finances renewable-energy systems for commercial and residential clients. After deregulated energy prices in the Chicago-land area caused home-energy prices to skyrocket, Dwyer has seen inquiries into renewable-energy systems jump from one a month to one a day.

Purchasing utility-traded renewable-energy credits (RECs) is a wonderful alternative for households with limited options for using solar or other renewable-energy sources but that want to support green power. The Department of Energy's National Renewable Energy Laboratory (www.nrel.gov) ranks the leading green-pricing programs, which hundreds of utilities around the nation now offer. Additionally, the Environmental Protection Agency (www.epa.gov) has a "Buying Green Power" link on its website featuring a green power provider locator for each state.

mcdonald-wucherer home

SANTA CRUZ, CALIFORNIA

Michael McDonald is a real estate agent at Coldwell Banker, and Vince Wucherer, a pastry chef by profession, is the head baker at the renowned Icing on the Cake Bakery in Los Gatos. Vince is also a certified redesigner—a design expert for those of us with no decorating ability—who reworks a home's preexisting furnishings in ways that work better with the interior space. + Michael says that as a young man he was drawn to music as a profession, but in his senior year of college he realized that his vocational opportunities lay elsewhere. A radical switch to computer science studies resulted in a Master's Degree and a promising career ahead.

Large panes of glass in the "turret" open up the living room to the sky. The slate used elsewhere in the home is repeated around the fireplace. The flooring is FSC-certified Brazilian cherry.

While enthusiastically spending eighteen years as a software engineer, he invested in real estate and soon discovered how much joy he found by remodeling and selling homes. Michael decided that these aspects of real estate were so rewarding that he wanted to do it for other people as well.

Michael's varied background of science, art, and real estate savvy served him well when it was time to find their dream home. He looked for a "crappy house in a great location," and after a year's search, they found the property in which he and Vince now live. They somehow saw past the formulaic one-story 1970s design and made an offer the same day. Unfortunately, the home located just down the street from scenic West Cliff Drive in Santa Cruz would need a second story before they could get the coveted ocean views.

The house was still in escrow when they interviewed architects Martha Matson and Cove Britton. The four of them clicked immediately and began to plan a 2,750-square-foot model of sustainability on the California coast. Vince and Michael envisioned an open, flowing floor plan centered on organic materials—stone, metal, glass, and wood—and they wanted an environment in tune with the stunning natural beauty outside their home. Structural and interior design elements would reflect the four elements of earth, air, fire, and water, from the skylights and fireplace to the choice of fabrics and cabinetry.

The couple's original plan was to have a master bedroom open to the living room below, but architects Matson and Britton convinced them to add wall-sized windows instead for maintaining their privacy when entertaining houseguests, while still being able to enjoy the dramatic views of Monterey Bay. Because the solar electricity was not part of the original plan, Matson and Britton designed the home for optimum

The McDonald-Wucherer home is filled with treasures from local artists, such as the glassware from Santa Cruz artist Ann Morhauser's Annieglass Ultramarine collection and original watercolors by Marie Gabrielle.

passive solar energy gain. The expansive windows and judicious use of skylights and dormers warm and light the home. When strategically opened, the windows, rooftop deck door, and skylights create a cooling airflow that requires no mechanical ventilation.

The home's seventeen net-metered solar panels were not part of initial construction but were added later by Solar Technologies in Santa Cruz. In their next project, Michael says they would use building-integrated PV (photovoltaic) strips—specifically the type with an adhesive backing to lay between the seams of a standing-seam roof, a roofing system that he as a real estate agent loves to see on homes in salty coastal environments like his.

Michael says his renewable-energy choices stem from a developing awareness that made him realize that the energy he used was spewing carbon dioxide, and every kilowatt of green energy they use helps them feel more responsible about their choices. Michael adds that part of a collective problem on this planet is that we all have to do our part; he and Vince looked at solar and said "we can afford to do it, we want to do it, it's the right thing to do, and it potentially adds value to our house."

ENERGY-CONSCIOUS LIFESTYLE TIP: PLUG AIR LEAKS

It seems simple, but the more a home is sealed, the fewer energy dollars it will take to keep it warm in winter and cool in summer. Begin by identifying and sealing air leaks around vents, chimneys, doors, windows, foundations, and where utility pipes enter the house. Stopping air leakage is the most cost-effective improvement you can make for reducing energy consumption.

Photovoltaic panels tucked away on an unseen roofline provide more than enough power for the home's needs.

AN INSIDER'S VIEW

Michael McDonald wisely advises homeowners to carefully choose their approach to sustainable living. You can do everything 100 percent green or you can take an easier road and accomplish the sustainable things that can be done immediately, he says. In the end, there is always a trade-off. For example, their use of solar panels balanced having some appliances that are not the most energy-efficient models available. "You can always do more," Michael says, "but you cannot build a house without waste or energy use, so don't let guilt stop your progress. Even off-grid homeowners must ask themselves, if you use batteries, are batteries green? It is a matter of searching your own conscience. In the final analysis, do what you can, do what works for you—only you know what is enough."

As the interior decorator, Vince handled the artwork and furniture for the home while Michael focused on the building materials. Together, they selected a combination of gray and olive 24 x 24-inch slate for the floor tiles. They debated at length between a gray and an olive tone before they came to the realization that they could choose both. Luckily, there was enough commonality in the earthy tones that they worked very well together. The cold material of the concrete and slate is deftly balanced with natural cherry-wood cabinets and FSC-certified Brazilian cherry hardwood floors. The green shades on the walls added warmth, as did the reds and browns used in accent pillows and elsewhere in the furnishings.

Michael says quite honestly that he and Vince are not avid gardeners but were interested in having a beautiful garden with the least amount of effort possible. Their solution, in a brilliant bit of detective work, was simply to walk the neighborhood to see which native plants thrived with little maintenance or watering. Their landscaping now includes Mediterranean herbs and succulents and a host of other low-maintenance vegetation.

Cove says that architecturally the McDonald-Wucherer challenge was primarily the location of the entrance. They had fabulous views out the front, and the back was a great hangout space that they did not want to disrupt, so they decided to put the front door in the middle of the house—something that at first met resistance from the local planning commission but was smoothed out by the architects. Dormers were added to control light coming into the house and to soften and reduce glare, which allowed the homeowners to obtain natural, even light from up high as opposed to skylights, which can cause hotspots.

GREAT GREEN FEATURES

- 9-kilowatt solar electric system
- FSC-certified Brazilian cherry hardwood floors
- Passive solar heating and cooling design
- Extensive use of natural light
- Low-maintenance xeriscaping around the home

chengson home
APTOS, CALIFORNIA

IN 2000, ENGINEERS DAVE AND LILLIAM CHENGSON bought a house with breathtaking Monterey Bay views with a desire to incorporate green features into their home from the very start. Unfortunately, the home, originally built in the late 1980s, was full of mold and mildew—with a major interior water leak that required immediate professional help before any green remodeling could be done. The couple had seen projects architect Martha Matson had done, and begged her and her husband Cove Britton to work with them. After a few false starts, Martha and Cove came onboard and, fortunately for the Chengsons, they are among the area's most innovative designers. From there on, Dave says, the project took on a life of its own.

RIGHT: Hydronic heating on both floors beneath slabs of marble keeps the bathroom warm year round. BELOW & FACING: For the wood flooring and finish work the Chengsons chose Lyptus, a fast growing, environmentally friendly eucalyptus hybrid.

Despite the problems, Lilliam and Dave saw one positive aspect in the solar orientation. The home faces perfectly south, but the sun only intrudes about a foot onto the marble floor at noon on the summer solstice, while the winter solstice lights up the back wall. The Chengsons decided to take advantage of all the home's green aspects that would give them a low-carbon footprint and allow them to utilize natural resources (especially water) as responsibly as possible. Dave had seen an article on rainwater catchment in *Fine Homebuilding*, which piqued his interest, and as an electrical engineer, he had always had an interest in solar power. Luckily, Monterey Bay tends to have winter sun and summer fog, which worked out well not only in moderating indoor temperatures but also in that roof-mounted solar collectors would pick up lots of solar energy when it was needed most.

For home heating, the architects added hydronic heating on both floors with marble slabs above the pipes. The Chengsons wanted to do green things with the woodwork as well. For the finished wood, Cove recommended Lyptus—a trade name of a hybrid of two species of eucalyptus—for its expansion properties and comparable cost to premium oak flooring. Intended for rapid harvesting on Brazilian plantations, the product is proposed as an environmentally conscious substitute for products taken from old-growth forests of oak, cherry, mahogany, and other woods. Besides maturing three times faster than similar hardwoods, the hardness rating of Lyptus is higher than red oak, considered the industry benchmark.

The Chengsons also installed a Galvalume Plus unpainted metal roof suitable for collecting

GREAT GREEN FEATURES

- 9-kilowatt photovoltaic system with 88 roof mounted solar panels with battery backup
- Rainwater catchment system with a 40,000-gallon underground cistern providing all potable domestic water year round
- Passive solar water heating
- Extensive use of renewable eucalyptus wood
- Energy-efficient CFL and LED lighting

In addition to Hüper Optik ceramic-based film on the windows to control solar gain, MechoShade motorized shades block the sun on the south side of the home when needed. Skylights can be opened to produce a chimney effect for drawing out excess heat in summer.

rainwater. The 6,000-square-foot metal roof feeds a 40,000-gallon underground cistern with an ultraviolet disinfection system able to sustain four people through a year-long drought. Despite several challenges in perfecting their rainwater catchment system, the Chengsons wanted to continue the project; in the end, it became a five-year journey to get it right. The water system is designed to capture rainwater for internal use only. For outside water applications, such as in the gardens, they use a community well. As California is trending to more drought and more wildfires, the Chengsons feel their water-conservation arrangement can only grow in value.

The solar aspect of the Chengsons renewable-energy system was more straightforward. Their system is grid-tied and produces more electricity than they consume, but Dave carefully uses a Kill A Watt meter to check everything from the toothbrush charger to the TV to their computers to minimize the power they consume. They purchased super-efficient LED bulbs on eBay for ambient background lighting to further reduce their energy load.

In an open floor plan with high ceilings, heat tends to gather near the ceiling, but in a radiant system objects in the home are heated in addition to the air. Forced-air heating super-heats the air, but in radiant heating not all the air escapes when you open a door—an obvious advantage, Cove says. Radiant heating is also better for allergy and chemical sensitivity issues because air is not blown around the house and there are no filters to change. To produce a chimney effect for reducing any overheating in summer, Cove came up with the solution of skylights. Dave Chengson came up with the idea of covering the skylights with black fabric to prevent hotspots. MechoShade motorized shades were also

ABOVE: Glass and steel spiral staircases that seem to float in space keep the interior open and filled with light. **RIGHT:** The 6,000 square-foot Galvalume Plus metal roof not only houses the home's solar collectors, it cleanly channels rain-water to a 40,000 gallon underground cistern.

added to block the sun on the wall of glass on the southern side of the home.

Dave reads his utility meter daily to track energy use, so when electric cars become available, he can figure out how to charge the car and not impact the household power supply. The Chengsons' other plans for the future include a methane digester, water storage in the great room, and perhaps more hydroponic food production to supplement the tomatoes and snow peas they now grow on a small scale. They are also considering wind power—particularly the new vertical-oriented turbines that look more like sculpture than energy generators.

ENERGY-CONSCIOUS LIFESTYLE TIP: INSULATE

Literally above all else, insulate your attic. About 40 percent of home heating is lost through the attic if it is not properly insulated. If you have less than a foot of insulation, you probably need more. Do not leave gaps or compress the insulation around plumbing and electrical conduits and make sure air leaks are well sealed before insulating.

The Chengsons use a community well shared with several neighbors to feed the gardens and Asian-influenced water features around the home such as this koi pond.

The husband-and-wife team of Cove Britton and Martha Matson says their clients really drive the green-building process. In effect, they show the clients the tools available and the homeowners guide them on how far to go. As for the future of green building, Martha and Cove see the growth of geothermal as a great way to handle home heating, and they also see more small-scale wind turbines being used in household applications. In addition, they expect to see more rainwater-collection systems put into use as water shortages increase. Economic systems using septic tank technology can be employed for lawn-and-garden irrigation and car washing for as little as $2,500, they say. Martha and Cove are strong advocates of modern architecture in homes because it offers the greenest potential. Cove points out that planting a PV system on the roof does not make a house green, but simplifying the home is a way to make it greener.

Martha and Cove also used Hüper Optik ceramic-based film from Germany, as opposed to most films, which are metal based, to control solar energy entering the house. Hüper Optik nanotechnology window films not only greatly reduce the total solar energy buildup in the house, but they also reduce more than 99.9 percent of ultraviolet rays. The nonreflective films have the added feature of low reflectivity at night so that the view is not obscured. It also provides significant heat reduction, lowering air-conditioning cooling load and energy consumption.

One cautionary note: Dave enjoys playing with the system and tweaking various parameters, and even though he is a highly trained electrical engineer, he advises others not to attempt a solar-energy system as a do-it-yourself project. Hire a professional installer, he says.

AN INSIDER'S VIEW

Dave Chengson recommends talking to as many people as possible who have actually done green building—and ride their learning curve. He encourages people to make a difference by simply experimenting on a smaller scale, perhaps not a 40,000-gallon cistern to save water, but a hardware-store garbage can for $15 filled with rainwater diverted by downspouts. If everyone did this, Dave says, the amount of rainwater effluent would be reduced substantially. In the end, he says, there are enough creative people to devise and improvise ways to make a difference for our planet.

wentworth
commons

CHICAGO, ILLINOIS

WHILE MOST OF THE HOMES in this book are single-family custom homes, it is important to note that inspirational solar homes can exist in any location and on any budget. Susan F. King, AIA, LEED AP, the architect in charge of the Wentworth Commons project, says that environmental concerns and the need for quality affordable housing are two of the most pressing issues of our time. As such, Wentworth Commons is an important part of a new movement that is raising the standard for affordable, sustainable building.

In spring 2001, Mercy Housing Lakefront, a not-for-profit developer of affordable housing, hired the century-old architectural firm of Harley Ellis Devereaux to design affordable apartments on an urban infill site on Chicago's South Side that would incorporate good energy-efficient design and low-maintenance materials. While sustainable or "green" design was a goal because it made sense, an energy-efficient building would mean lower-operating costs. The result was the first LEED-certified multiunit residential building in Illinois.

Completed in October 2005, the Wentworth Commons Residence provides fifty-one apartments for recently homeless or at-risk families and individuals in the Roseland neighborhood of Chicago. The 65,800-square-foot, four-story building has a housing program on the upper floors and supportive services, including a family resource center with community space, case management areas, employment training, and leadership development on the ground floor. Apartments range in size from studios to four bedrooms and are blended throughout the building, creating a sense of community.

King's Life Enhancement design team at Harley Ellis Devereaux strived to create an environment with the feel and function of a home by providing residents with the proper balance of privacy and community. The Wentworth is served by two major bus lines, one of which provides connections to a commuter rail station one mile east of the building. The project is pedestrian and bicycle friendly, with a permanent bike storage room on the ground floor for resident and staff use.

The most obvious green feature is the 33-kilowatt-per-hour rooftop photovoltaic array, which, rather than being hidden away, is celebrated as part of the

ENERGY-CONSCIOUS LIFESTYLE TIP: GET LOW-FLOW FAUCETS AND SHOWERHEADS

In the average home, the amount of energy spent in heating water is surpassed only by energy use for heating and cooling. Low-flow showerheads and faucet aerators can lessen water-heating expenses. Also consider using cold water for laundry and automatic dishwashing. Always do full loads, use the water- and energy-saver settings, and air dry as much as possible. If your home is on a private well, saving water will reduce electric-pump use, often a large energy drain.

building's design. On peak days, the sun provides around 20 percent of the building's energy needs. The mechanical system is considerably more efficient than those typically seen in this type of building, including a heat-recovery unit and building-automation system that allows the owner to carefully control the energy use of the building systems.

Materials and products were selected based on evaluating different aspects of content and location of manufacturing. Preference was given to locally made products, those that contained either recycled content, or those made from rapidly renewable sources. In fact, 26 percent of the building products were manufactured within a 500-mile radius of the project, including all exterior masonry. The Astra-Glaze product that gives the exterior its lively color was in part selected because of its graffiti-resistant properties.

In terms of having a low impact on the city's existing combined sewer and storm infrastructure,

Wentworth Commons won Harley Ellis Devereaux the 2006 Show You're Green award from the National American Institute of Architects' Housing Committee for excellence in the design of "green" housing. Astra-Glaze pre-faced architectural concrete masonry blocks used for the exterior have a thermosetting glazing compound permanently molded to one or more faces that make them graffiti-resistant.

storm-water management was addressed through native or climate-tolerant plantings arranged in bio-swales and rain gardens. A unique landscape design moderates the quantity of and the time it takes storm water to enter the city's storm systems. In addition, the urban heat-island effect is further reduced through highly reflective paving and a white roof.

Architect Susan King says her mission is changing the definition of affordable housing and the funding mechanisms for providing it. She says that the fundamental flaw in today's definition of "affordable" is that it only applies to initial building cost. Payback has to be part of the formula, but this definition needs to expand to include long-term operating cost. This is as true for single-family homes as it is for multi-unit buildings like Wentworth Commons.

AN INSIDER'S VIEW

Susan F. King, AIA, LEED AP, principal architect for Wentworth Commons, advises that when sustainability is the goal, incorporating it as early as possible in the design process is crucial. With the Wentworth project, sustainability was identified during the initial feasibility study, and she believes this early commitment contributed to its success as an award-winning green building.

roof gardens, geothermal well, eco-friendly

riverhouse at one rockefeller park

NEW YORK, NEW YORK

WITH RIVERHOUSE IN NEW YORK CITY, the Sheldrake Organization set out to create the East Coast's greenest condominium. At the time of this writing, the design team is striving to achieve LEED Platinum certification from the U.S. Green Building Council. The LEED Green Building Rating System is a nationally standardized set of criteria for assessing and developing high-performance, sustainable buildings. In exceeding LEED's gold rating, the stunning 32-story, 264-unit luxury condominium overlooking the Hudson River incorporates groundbreaking technology and world-class design to set a metropolitan standard for sustainable living.

Riverhouse, a premiere LEED Gold luxury condominium, delivers the highest-performance green living standards ever offered in condominium housing in Manhattan. Its East Lobby also features a 900-gallon salt water aquarium.

From its innovative double-glazed curtain wall to its geothermal well sunk deep into Manhattan's granite bedrock to its landscaped roof gardens above, the environmental performance of Riverhouse far exceeded that of any other residential development on the East Coast when it opened in spring 2008. The Sheldrake Organization, originally founded by J. Christopher Daly in 1988 to redevelop blighted properties in Hempstead, New York, strived to build an intelligent high-performance building that would not only raise the bar for green design but would also be an exceptional place to live.

The exterior architect, Polshek Partnership, designed a distinct exterior for Riverhouse that capitalized on the breathtaking waterfront views, while still delivering the highest level of energy efficiency. Polshek's solution was a dramatic U-shaped structure featuring a double-glazed curtain wall rarely seen in residential design with vast floor-to-ceiling windows in many of the residences with greater energy efficiency than traditional windows.

ENERGY-CONSCIOUS LIFESTYLE TIP: LOOK FOR THE ENERGY STAR

Energy Star products, which range from washing machines and freezers to air conditioners and water heaters, are measured against minimum federal efficiency standards, and the yearly savings differ depending on the appliance. The Energy Star label allows easy identification of the most energy-efficient products but also compares energy use among similar models using the familiar yellow Energy Guide stickers. For every dollar spent replacing inefficient appliances, you reduce by three to five dollars renewable-energy system costs needed to power them.

Riverhouse interiors, by internationally acclaimed designer David Rockwell, incorporate green building principles and renewable materials to create beautiful, high-performance living spaces.

Interiors designed by David Rockwell incorporate green-building principles and renewable materials to create beautiful high-performance living spaces. The design mission was openness and simplicity— blurring the boundary between the building and the

outside environment to create intelligently designed, eco-friendly, and uncluttered interiors. The one- to five-bedroom residences, with layouts by Ismael Leyva Architects, feature programmable thermostats; filtered air and water; water-saving faucets and fixtures; low- or no-emissions paints, adhesives, and sealants; and certified renewable and responsibly harvested woods.

In addition to its eco-conscious design, Riverhouse offers residents and the surrounding

Riverhouse, a 32-Story, 264-Unit waterfront luxury condominium in Battery Park City, New York, features triple pane glass windows and a glazed curtain wall to prevent heat loss in winter and maximize cooling in summer, effectively reducing the need to rely heavily on electrical heating and cooling sources.

GREAT GREEN FEATURES

- Standing-column geothermal well—The geothermal well uses the stable temperature of the earth and deep ground water to provide heating and cooling for the lobby spaces.
- Planted roof areas—Riverhouse has the highest percentage of green roof space in New York City, which helps to reduce storm-water runoff and to control ambient temperatures.
- Renewable energy generation—Photovoltaic modules mounted atop the roof produce solar energy, reducing the burden on public utilities.
- Cogeneration—One 60-kilowatt micro-turbine will produce electricity from natural gas and recover the excess heat for space heating and domestic hot water.
- Double-pane glass in windows—Low-e coating with thermally broken aluminum window frames prevent heat gain/loss.
- Condensing coil reheat—This recovers heat produced as a by-product of dehumidification during mild weather to temper outside air.
- Blackwater treatment facility and recapture of storm-water runoff—Facility recycles wastewater for the cooling tower and irrigation as well as significantly reduces potable water consumption.
- Condensing boilers—Modulating flames heat water with 90 percent efficiency.
- Eco-friendly construction—Regionally, available materials are used wherever possible to reduce fuel consumed during shipping.
- Twenty-four-hour oxygen filtration—Preconditioned air is supplied to all apartments.

community an incredible array of amenities, such as lower Manhattan's first branch of the New York Public Library and its very own organic café, City Bakery. Riverhouse will also be the new home of Poets House, an educational literary center and archive containing more than 45,000 volumes of poetry. The building will also wrap around a new extension of Tear Drop Park, an Adirondacks-inspired public space designed by Michael Van Valkenburgh.

On-site parking with reserved spaces for low-emission cars will be available as well as bicycle and kayak storage.

GREAT GREEN DESIGN ELEMENTS

- Main lobby features spiral staircase with reclaimed wood floor treads and handrails
- Reclaimed teak flooring and column bases made from railway ties from Southeast Asia with water-based finishes
- Walls feature custom-plaster finish made from natural mineral pigments
- Entry features recycled-aluminum floor grates
- Rooftop photovoltaic louvers used that annually produce 42,154 kilowatts of useable energy
- Carpet made from recycled materials
- Vertical-grain amber bamboo flooring featured
- Custom-designed teak entry door hardware used
- Use of recycled and reclaimed materials creates cleaner air during construction (new materials emit toxic gases)
- Benjamin Moore low-VOC and low-odor EcoSpec paint used throughout
- Kitchens feature Energy Star–compliant Sub-Zero refrigerators, Miele dishwashers, and recirculating hoods

florence lofts

SEBASTOPOL, CALIFORNIA

BUILT BY IBIS (INTELLIGENT BUILDING = INTEGRATED + SUSTAINABLE), the Florence Lofts were en-visioned by three partners as an environmentally friendly and sustainable live/work development that integrates a sense of community as well as respect for renewable resources. Joe Marshall and Robert Nissenbaum, founder and CEO of Imagine Foods, both worked in the natural organic foods industry. Nissenbaum is also vice chair of the board of Stirling Energy Systems, a company behind the two largest solar-power-generating plants in the world. Architect Steven Sheldon has been a green general contractor and developer in Sonoma County for the last thirty years.

The light-filled main living area features FSC-certified built-in cabinetry, bamboo stairs, and radiant heat–warmed concrete floors.

DECODING LEED FOR HOMES

LEED for Homes (LEED-H) awards points in eight categories for building practices and materials or product choices. All LEED-program homes have to implement eighteen obligatory procedures. Additionally, sixteen points must be earned to meet the minimum prerequisites in four categories. Architects and builders can decide how to obtain additional points depending on such factors as owner budget, home design, local climate, and building site. Below are the LEED categories and total points available.

Innovation and Design—Integrating understanding of all the construction trades in the design process, planning to make the most long-lasting house possible, and orienting the house for solar design. (11 points)

Locations and Linkages—Selecting a socially and environmentally responsible site. (10 points)

Sustainable Sites—Minimizing the impact of construction and the home on the site. (22 points)

Water Efficiency—Conserving indoor and outdoor water. (15 points)

Energy and Atmosphere—Constructing a tight, well-insulated building envelope with efficient heating and cooling systems. (38 points)

Materials and Resources—Reducing product waste during construction while using green materials. (16 points)

Indoor Environmental Quality—Using appliances, installation methods, and ventilation procedures for improving indoor air quality. (21 points)

Awareness and Education—Compiling a homeowner's manual for covering the ongoing operation and maintenance of the home. (3 points)

The gourmet kitchens feature Paperstone countertops, Energy Star appliances and custom FSC-certified maple veneer Europly cabinets from Columbia Forest Products.

The core principals of Sheldon's designs include: energy efficiency and conservation of resources; economy of space while creating a sense of openness; utilization of natural light; and the integration of buildings with their surrounding landscape.

The Florence Lofts project focuses on three elements: (1) energy—in the form of solar design, on-site power generation with building-integrated photovoltaics, and energy-efficient appliances; (2) water conservation—by recycling 150,000 gallons of gray water per year for landscape irrigation, by allowing stormwater to permeate back into the aquifer by ensuring that all areas of the site not covered by buildings are permeable, and by installing water conserving fixtures; and (3) using green, sustainable

BELOW: The ground floor open office spaces feature radiant heat concrete floors, energy efficient lighting and an abundance of dual-paned low-e glazed windows so no artificial lighting is needed during sunny days. FACING: The cozy loft bedrooms boast FSC-certified built-in cabinetry and bamboo flooring.

building materials. The designers were also looking to create higher-density living, but with spaces that are light and airy in an effort to maintain human dignity. Five blocks from downtown Sebastopol in the Sonoma County wine country of Northern California, Florence Lofts includes twelve live/work townhouses with an adjoining commercial building with retail space, offices, and a restaurant/deli.

Interiors are designed with daily life in mind by providing separate yet adjacent living-and-working spaces. Exterior areas are designed to be peaceful community spaces in the midst of town. The live/

AN INSIDER'S VIEW

Florence Lofts architect Steven Sheldon has been focused on green building throughout his entire career—buildings with a natural relationship with the environment as opposed to confronting the natural environment. Sheldon says this is always what he has done—use passive solar first and then use as little energy as possible. Even before the pressure of saving energy in homebuilding emerged in recent years, if a building could heat and cool itself through its design, it just made sense to do it, he says. Sheldon sees solar building as an opportunity for creating a form that has a rational purpose rather than a superimposed aesthetic following a current trend.

work concept is the foundation of the Florence project, which is close to services, and an easy walk to downtown Sebastopol. The twelve townhouses have professional office space on the ground floor for independent practitioners featuring a 650-square-foot space with high ceilings and a separate entrance. The second floor features living, dining, and kitchen spaces, while the third floor holds a sleeping loft for a total of 880 square feet of living space. Sheldon says much of the current focus of green building and sustainable design has to do with downsizing— moving into an urban context as driving becomes more expensive. The high-end amenities and materials were designed for people following the downsizing trend and empty nesters. The Florence Lofts are also designed with cabinets and storage built in so that less furniture is needed. Sheldon notes that in-fill projects such as this have not historically been as affected by downturns in the economy.

At Florence Lofts, the sun conditions the thermal environment. Achieving perfect solar orientation is often a challenge with multifamily dwellings, but all of the townhouses are oriented south or southwest. Windows are shaded in summer but oriented for solar passive gain in winter. A solar thermal system heats slabs on the ground and second floors, which also act as thermal mass. All roofs are covered in building-integrated photovoltaic (BIPV) material.

Exterior balconies and trellis work will soon be covered in lush gray-water irrigated foliage. The balconies and trellis work are intentionally rusted and designed to support the deciduous vines that will shade windows during the hotter summer months.

Interiors are designed to allow ample daylight for working and living activities. Proper cross ventilation is ensured with operable windows that have energy-efficient Low-E2 glazing (also called "solar control glass"). The windows are located to allow solar heat gain in the winter and are shaded in the summer months. In-floor radiant heat provides comfort at lower air temperatures.

Many of the products used in building Florence Lofts are of high-recycled-material content. The steel framing of all building walls consists of up to 80 percent recycled steel. Concrete substitutes 15 to 50 percent fly ash for cement. The wood used for construction is FSC certified from sustainably managed forests. Additionally, all materials were selected to minimize the need for maintenance over the life of the building.

Through an arrangement with a local mortgage company, JCF Advisors, credits that offset Global Climate Change (called "carbon credits") will be purchased and retired in the owner's name through Carbonfund.org. JCF Advisors will offset 100 percent of the global-warming emissions produced for two years.

However, Sheldon emphasizes that solar is only one aspect of living sustainably. Because buildings consume nearly 50 percent of our energy and create 40 percent of CO_2, hundreds of small things, from turning off the water while shaving or brushing teeth to maintaining proper tire pressure on your car, are important. He also stresses that we have to look not only at building materials, but practices of the building-products manufacturers, and must support those with a strong environmental consciousness. Buying local to limit transportation impact is also an important consideration.

GREAT GREEN FEATURES

General

- Complete integration of landscaping with all buildings
- Gray-water recirculation for landscape irrigation
- Bio-remediation (biological cleansing) of storm-water runoff
- Short walking distance to downtown area, parks, and public transportation

Design

- Attractive integration of landscaping features and all buildings
- Community courtyard with water flows and landscaping
- On-site electricity generation from building integrated photovoltaic panels (BIPVs)
- Gray-water recirculation for irrigation
- Permeable pavement throughout site for groundwater retention and reduced storm-water runoff
- Convenient walk to downtown parks, shopping, entertainment, and public transportation
- Ninety-seven percent efficient on-demand heating/hot-water boiler
- Breathable no-VOC clay paint
- Energy-efficient dimmable lighting
- Bamboo flooring in the stairs and loft
- Energy Star ceiling fans

Bathrooms

- Colored-cement vanity top and tub surround in master bathroom
- Dual-flush toilets
- Ultra-low-flow showerhead: 1.5 gpm

Kitchen

- Bosch Energy Star stainless-steel dishwashers
- Custom-made cabinets with FSC-certified wood
- Paperstone recycled-paper/resin countertop
- Low-noise stainless-steel range hood

natural cooling,
open design,
cost effective,
visual corridor...

solar umbrella

VENICE, CALIFORNIA

IN 1993, LAWRENCE SCARPA walked into his office and saw a piece of blue glass sitting on his desk, and asked, "What the heck is that?" It turned out that it was a solar panel. Scarpa thought it was incredibly beautiful, which rekindled an interest in the architectural work he had done as a graduate student. He has been devoted to sustainable architecture ever since. + Lawrence Scarpa and Angela Brooks, both architects with the firm Pugh+Scarpa, grew up in Florida and early in their careers worked for Paul Rudolph, famed designer of the iconic 1950s Umbrella House in Sarasota, which used a canopy to shade the house and jalousie windows to catch prevailing winds for natural

cooling. Inspired by Rudolph's Umbrella House, Lawrence and his wife Angela's Solar Umbrella home in California features a contemporary reinvention of the solar canopy—a strategy that provides thermal protection in climates with intense sun—while using photovoltaic panels for shade and to provide 95 percent of the home's energy needs. In addition to a host of other awards, it was voted one of the American Institute of Architects' Top Ten Green Projects of 2006.

Along with the photovoltaic solar panel array, the home's green aspects include solar hot-water-heating panels, a storm-water retention system, and an airy, open design with environmentally sound materials used throughout. Many of the material finishes are highly unconventional: eco-friendly and cost-effective building materials that are traditionally hidden from view are repositioned here as unusual and aesthetically appealing design elements.

Settled in a neighborhood of single-story bungalows in Venice, California, the Solar Umbrella residence boldly establishes a precedent for the next generation of California modernist architecture. Located on a 41 x 100-foot through lot, the Solar Umbrella addition transformed the architects' existing 650-square-foot 1920s bungalow into a

1,900-square-foot residence equipped for responsible living in the twenty-first century. Recycled, renewable, and high-performance materials and products are used throughout the home, and hardscape (ponds, garden walls, patios, and pathways) and landscape treatments were considered for their aesthetic and actual impact on the land.

Taking advantage of the unusual through-lot site, the renovation shifted the residence 180 degrees. What was formerly the front and main entry at the north became the back as the new design reoriented the residence toward the south. This allowed Brooks

MEASURING GREEN-BUILDING COSTS

There is considerable disagreement between green architects and builders and even green homeowners about whether sustainable homes cost more than conventional ones. Some estimate that building green adds anywhere from 5 to 15 percent to construction costs while many maintain that when resale value, lifecycle cost, and the longer life span that are typical in higher-quality homes are factored in, there is no additional cost and even a savings. Nevertheless, a major factor that is rarely considered when renewable-energy systems are involved is taxes. In most locales, there are no sales and property taxes on renewable-energy systems.

recycled, renewable, and high-performance materials
and products are used throughout the home

Floating, folded-plate steel stairs above the open living area lead to the master bedroom. Oriented Strand Board (OSB), an environmentally friendly product made from wood scraps, is the primary flooring material.

and Scarpa a more gracious introduction to their residence and optimized their solar panels' exposure to energy-rich sunlight while offering a bold artistic display of the blue glass that captivated Lawrence years ago. As a solar canopy, these panels protect the body of the building from thermal heat gain by screening large portions of the structure from direct exposure to the intense Southern California sun. Like many design features at the Solar Umbrella, the solar canopy performs several roles for both function and aesthetic impact.

The original bungalow, which was tightly packed with kitchen, dining, living, bedroom, and bath spaces, now includes a new entry, living area, master suite, and utility room for laundry and storage. The kitchen, which once formed the back edge of the residence, opens into a large living area, which, in turn, opens out to a spacious front yard. An operable wall of glass at the living area elegantly defines the edge between interior and exterior, establishing an unbroken visual corridor from one end of the property to the other. Taking cues from the California modernist tradition, the homeowners envision exterior spaces as outdoor rooms and created strong visual and physical links between outside and inside. A cascading concrete pool provides a strong landscape element and defines the path to the front entry. In a reinvention of the welcome mat, stepping-stones immersed in the water create a playful passage into the residence, where the visitor is invited to walk across water. Angela has tracked their energy usage from day one and regularly fine-tunes the pump, pools, and ponds to increase their performance.

The master suite on the second level repeats the interlocking space design. Located directly above the new living area, up a set of floating, folded-plate steel stairs, the bedroom strategically opens onto a deep, covered patio overlooking the garden. This patio in effect extends the bedroom area outdoors, creating the sensation of a sleeping loft exposed to the open air.

Completed in April 2005, the structure appears to sit lightly upon the land with light penetrating the interior of the residence at several locations. A series of stepped roofs, glazed walls, and clerestory windows broadcast light from multiple directions. Solar panels provide shelter and establish a distinctive architectural expression. Homosote, an acoustical wall panel made from recycled newspaper, is used as a finish material for custom cabinets. Oriented strand board (OSB), a structural-grade building material formed from scrap wood, is the primary flooring material where concrete is not used, providing a cost-effective and environmentally responsible alternative to hardwood. Metal-stud construction replaces conventional wood framing. Recycled-steel panels, solar-powered in-floor radiant heating, and high-efficiency appliances and fixtures as well as low-VOC paint replaced conventional materials. Decomposed granite and gravel hardscape, including a storm-water retention basin, are used in place of concrete or stone outdoors, allowing the ground to absorb water, mitigating urban runoff to the nearby ocean. Drought-tolerant xeriscaping complements the textures and palette of the building while providing a low-maintenance, aesthetically appealing landscape.

GREEN GREEN FEATURES

- Over 85 percent of the construction debris was recycled.
- Stucco used on the exterior has an integral colored pigment so that painting is never required.
- All concrete forming materials and 20 percent of the framing material are from reclaimed sources.
- Formaldehyde-free MDF (medium-density fiberboard) was used for the bedroom cabinets. Homosote (100 percent recycled newsprint) was used as a wall finish.
- All paint used is low VOC.

Operable skylights are used in the kitchen for natural light and ventilation and lighting control systems further reduce electric consumption. Appliances were carefully selected for both energy efficiency and water conservation.

The project's storm-water retention system retains 80 percent of roof storm water on-site, virtually unheard of for a project in the area. While most structures in the area have as much as 90 percent of their sites covered with nonpermeable surfaces, this project maintains over 65 percent of the site unpaved or landscaped on a lot that is only 4,100 square feet, dramatically reducing heat-island effects and runoff.

Operable windows and a perforated-steel stair are strategically placed so that as hot air rises, it passes through and out of the house. The rooms are kept cool with a combination of window placement for cross ventilation; double-glazed, krypton-filled, low-e windows with stainless-steel spacers; and recycled insulation that boosts the thermal value of the wall to 75 percent above a conventional wood-frame wall construction, which reduces envelope infiltration. Operable skylights are used in both the kitchen and a bathroom for natural light and ventilation and to maintain privacy.

Appliances were chosen for both energy efficiency and water conservation. The front-loading clothes washer and the dishwasher both use less water than traditional models. The kitchen faucet, showerheads, and toilets are all low-flow fixtures. The existing house toilet was replaced with a new low-flow type through a city rebate program at no cost to the owner.

Efficient use of space was seen as important: some of the furniture is built-in as in the kids' bedroom and the large couch in the living room (which allows storage to be built into the furniture). The living room couch is sized so that a portion of it can be used as a queen-sized bed for overnight guests. In the master bedroom on the second floor, the wall becomes the storage: a built-in wall of cabinets conceals clothes and drawers and the individual lighting for the bed.

The eighty-nine amorphous silicon solar panels in their 4.5-kilowatt system are net-metered by the City of Los Angeles, allowing the grid to be used as a storage system and eliminating the time-of-use charges with traditional electric use. Three solar hot water panels on the roof preheat the domestic hot water before it gets to the gas-fired hot water heater, and also heat the pool. These solar panels have cut the house's natural gas use 50 percent despite increasing the home 2.5 times its original size. Heat is provided through a radiant in-floor heating system for the concrete floors of the new addition. Heat through the floor is a more efficient mode of heating than through forced air, allowing for lower air temperatures and less energy usage.

One hundred percent of the house is day lit and requires no electric light except at night and on overcast days. Appliances are Energy Star rated and use substantially less energy than other models. Lighting control systems are used inside and out to further reduce consumption. Because of the very low power demand of the building, thousands of feet of wire were saved.

A key strategy was to provide extra insulation and to ensure minimal infiltration. A tight envelope resulted in a dramatically reduced demand for energy, therefore reducing the need and costs for systems that would have been necessary to produce more energy. Another important aspect for the owners and architects was the education of others regarding sustainable design. Several tours and events have been held at the house for other architects, design professionals, contractors, community organizations, and institutions. The owners hope to demystify sustainable design by demonstrating that it can be accomplished with little difficulty.

THE BOTTOM LINE

The city department of water and power provided a rebate of over $18,600 and the federal government provided a rebate of $4,000 for the solar system. Appliance rebates were $300. The remaining cost of the solar system was still substantial, about $20,000. The payback time on this is estimated to be twelve years. The solar hot water, which preheats the gas-fired water heater, has a payback time of ten years. Energy costs for the entire building are now less than $300 per year.

AN INSIDER'S VIEW

Lawrence Scarpa argues that a building that everyone loves that is an energy hog is more sustainable than a building that uses no energy but nobody likes because it would soon be torn down and replaced. Their goal was to create beautiful low-maintenance high-quality architecture that is sustainable. The Solar Umbrella, both beautiful and energy generating, will continue to serve that purpose long into the future. As we continue to see utility prices rise, the solar panels will become even more important, he says. Lawrence and Angela believe showcasing solar panels in a way that lets people see they can be beautiful and serve a dual purpose has far-reaching and long-lasting effects. They say the most important intelligent-design strategy is proper planning and orientation, making your home as passively sustainable as possible. Active systems then become icing on the cake.

poured earth, reflector decks, integrated solar

frerking home

PRESCOTT, ARIZONA

ARIZONA ARCHITECT AND BUILDER MICHAEL FRERKING is passionate about using on-site and local renewable resources to create affordable green homes. He is also a fervent advocate for the use of fly
ash, an industrial waste product. Frerking's enthusiasm for this seemingly unpleasant product stems
from its role as a temporary bridge to greening the manufacture of concrete, a building material traditionally high in embodied energy. Scrubbed from coal and similar in appearance to Portland cement,
fly ash produces a higher-quality concrete than the conventional material. Michael, owner of Prescott-
based Living Systems Architecture and Construction and the Living Systems Building Group, has

The Frerking home's sixteen-inch thick poured earth walls moderate Arizona's extremes of heat and cold while careful attention to glazing allows aesthetically and psychologically pleasing use of daylight.

FINDING PV AND SOLAR HOT WATER SYSTEM DEALERS

Contact your local Solar Energy Industries Association chapter (www.seia.org) or the chapter of the American Solar Energy Society (www.ases.org) in your state. If your state lacks a chapter, a neighboring state's chapter may have a distributor who also works in your state or can offer referrals to qualified dealers. Your system retailer should recommend a reputable installer if they don't offer that service. A quality installer will belong to a state or regional Solar Energy Industries Association chapter or the national association.

been designing and building earth homes and buildings since 1975 but saw fly ash as a way to make the "poured earth" homes he builds that much stronger and greener.

Poured earth (also known as "poured soil cement") is a new method for the ancient process of using earth as a building material. Continuing the age-old tradition, modern earth builders primarily work in adobe and rammed earth, which require considerable time and labor. Poured-earth buildings with sixteen-inch-wide walls, however, can be built in the same amount of time as standard construction.

Michael and Joanne Frerking's own energy-efficient poured-earth home is carefully constructed against a hillside, using the surrounding earth's constant temperature to moderate Arizona's extremes of hot and cold. Windows are positioned to allow the low winter sun to enter deep into the home, where the floors and walls absorb the heat and release it slowly at night. Wide overhangs and a well-insulated roof shelter the interior from the summer heat. Twenty-inch walls with a four-inch rigid foam thermal break in the center provide over 200 tons of mass to moderate temperatures inside the home.

Currently, the cost to build a cast-earth home is comparable to that of adobe and rammed earth. According to Frerking, building a 2,000-square-foot cast-earth house costs 10 to 15 percent more than a comparable stick-built house, but homeowners quickly recoup those costs in lower utility bills. He says an added bonus is increased building longevity, as his homes are designed to last hundreds of years versus present minimum standard construction that has a likely lifetime of 25 to 75 years. Frerking says that to have a poured-earth home, your region should have at least 50 percent sunny days during winter; and for cooling, daily temperature swings should vary between more than twenty and thirty degrees Fahrenheit.

After ten years of working with adobe and ten years with rammed earth, Michael began using poured earth in 1995. Unlike rammed-earth homes, where you can only install twenty yards a day, with poured earth you can do a minimum of twenty yards an hour. Frerking hopes this will lead to an economy of scale that will allow more people to live in these energy-efficient and healthy homes. Frerking's ultimate dream is for products like poured earth to be used in middle-market homes—something he does not see adobe and rammed earth doing because of the lower efficiency of production and high labor requirements.

Windows are skillfully placed to allow winter sun to enter deeply into the home while wide overhangs and a well-insulated roof shelter the interior spaces from extreme desert heat.

AN INSIDER'S VIEW

Michael Frerking's advice? Hire people with significant experience in designing and building green—lots of people who have turned green overnight will not have the education or know-how to provide you with a green home. Michael adds that the most successful green homes—even if they do not go all the way with every possible sustainable option—are the ones where the homeowner made a decision to pick proven technologies with a reasonable payback period. Also, he says, seek out design/build groups with a track record for building the type of quality home you desire.

In addition to passive heating and cooling, Frerking's roof-mounted photovoltaic array supplies most of the home's electricity. A rooftop rainwater catchment system will store 10,000 gallons of runoff in a cistern for potable water, as well as for landscaping. Even with low rainfall of 10 inches per year, he can collect 30,000 gallons a year.

Built in 2003, the 3,800-square-foot home and office took ten months to construct. They devoted 1,300 feet of that area to studio and office space. Joanne, textile artist and co-owner of the Van Gogh's Ear art gallery in Prescott needed a home studio, and Michael has worked from home for thirty-five years. Michael is not an advocate for big homes, but when he and Joanne weighed the carbon footprint of commuting in their cars versus the carbon footprint of working from their house, a home office proved to be more energy efficient. They say it doesn't make environmental or economic sense to build a huge

Clerestory windows and "reflector decks" cast light deeply and evenly into the interior spaces where they are most needed—such as the kitchen.

LEARNING TO LOVE FLY ASH

Concrete was first produced by the ancient Romans using a mix of volcanic fly ash and lime. Today, fly ash is still available as "natural" volcanic fly ash or produced synthetically as a waste product from coal-fired power plants as well as from rice hulls. It is estimated that Portland cement production contributes as much as seven percent toward global climate change. However, when fly ash is added to the poured-earth mixture, the amount of Portland cement required can be reduced drastically, thereby presenting a method of creating much greener homes.

home if you are retired or have a small family, but in circumstances like theirs, larger homes can be more cost-effective.

The Frerking home's "reflector decks" are what Michael calls his signature passive solar design method. He used clerestory windows that are smaller but with a spectral reflector deck in front of them that is bent concave so the low winter sun doubles the amount of energy coming into the upper windows. These reflectors cast light into the thirty-foot-deep building, and in winter they throw light onto the ceiling, where it is reflected evenly across the floors and walls. Michael cautions that these must be carefully designed and installed by a trained professional because the intensely focused solar energy could present the danger of fire. Unlike the overglazed 1970s solar homes and their resulting high-temperature fluctuations from day and night, the art of what Frerking is doing is introducing high levels of light into a home for heat storage in the building's mass but doing it in a way that is aesthetically and psychologically pleasing, an aspect he says is not considered enough. Many passive solar buildings have mass, he says, but few

Recycled skeleton plates left over from industrial steel cutting provide security and "unintentional art" in the master bedroom. The doors are fitted with double-walled polycarbonate and have more than twice the R value of high performance glass.

have appropriate systems to get light in, distribute it evenly, and at the same time keep the home really comfortable. The end result is that poorly designed passive solar homes do not recoup the added cost of high mass through energy savings.

Because the Frerkings wanted to build in a pristine hilltop area with a pine forest and scattered oak trees, building sizing and proper home siting were critical. Theirs is a sloping, heavily bouldered site, and in Michael's words, the house was built in "the worst spot on the property" to preserve the beauty of the land. You can simply walk up to the hilltop to get an effect of the views, and from a mile away you really have a hard time picking the home out of the surroundings because of its earthen coloration and the use of light and shadow in the home's design. In addition, it doesn't break the ridgeline like most homes in the area.

The Frerking's three-kilowatt solar-electric system not only provides 70 percent of their energy but the thin-film PV is integrated into the curving roof and does not protrude intrusively. Integrating the PV with the building has only a minimal effect on collector efficiency, Frerking says. He feels that the renewable-energy world is still suffering from the

perception that solar is unsightly, so showing his clients how well it can be integrated into a beautiful home was very important.

As an artist and gallery owner, Joanne's primary criterion for the house was that it would be an "art gallery in disguise." There had to be enough walls for art. Joanne also has a great sense of color, and because of the character of concrete and earth walls, they were able to do very unique wall finishes with varying textures. Rich hues and striking designs can be created by mixing natural pigments with the pale cast earth. The twenty-foot-high walls are a combination of poured concrete for the first ten feet and poured earth for the top half. Michael framed the interior walls with steel studs because at the time he built—before it tripled in price—the steel was cheap, had probably been recycled once or twice already, and caused little waste. They also used some local native woods, such as the hefty pine poles cut down while making a roadway in Flagstaff. A thermal break in the walls came in the form of 4 x 8 structural Styrofoam Tridipanels.

Passive solar homes use lots of venting, and homeowners ideally need to leave doors and windows open at night, but they need a reasonable

GREAT GREEN FEATURES

- Made of energy-efficient, passive solar poured-earth construction
- Three kilowatt building-integrated photovoltaic array supplies 70 percent of electricity
- Rooftop rainwater catchment system will store 30,000 gallons per year of runoff in a cistern for potable water and landscaping
- Reflector decks provide sunlight and passive solar heat
- Passive cooling and heating includes southern orientation, super low emissivity windows, and high thermal mass in slab and walls
- Radiant floor slab heated by solar hot water panels and excess voltage from the hydroelectric system

amount of security. Michael's answer for his own home was a waste-stream product called skeleton plates, which are left over when widgets are cut from 4 x 8-foot sheets of inch-thick steel. The "unintentional art" results in a beautiful insulating door that in winter is fitted with lightweight, translucent panel that allows 40 percent light transmission. The panels are double-walled polycarbonate and are injected with a product called nanogel that has an insulation value of R-8 per inch compared to "high performance glass" which has an R-3 value.

CREDITS

Architects, Designers, and Builders
Alma Designs
Boulder, CO
starek@almadesigns.com

American Renewable Energy
848 Dodge Ave., Suite 388
Chicago, IL 60202
847.594.5293
847.594.8794 (fax)
info@americanrenewable.com
www.americanrenewable.com

Craig Henritzy, Architect
8 Indian Rock Path
Berkeley, CA
510.526.8602
henritzy@mindspring.com
www.henritzy.com

Davis Frame Company
513 River Road
P.O. Box 1079
Claremont, NH 03743
800.636.0993
www.davisframe.com

Dewey + Associates, Architects
and Planners
P.O. Box 612
Londonderry, VT 05148
802.824.5612
deweyaia@sover.net

Gozzi Development, Inc.
P.O. Box 223808
Carmel, CA 93922
831.899.8692
831.394.1553 (fax)
info@gozzidevelopment.com
www.gozzidevelopment.com

Green Power Blue Collar
Chicago, IL
847.594.5293
info@greenpowerbluecollar.com
www.greenpowerbluecollar.com

Harley Ellis Devereaux
401 West Superior
Chicago, IL 60654
312.951.8863
312.951.1719 (fax)
www.hedev.com

IBIS
7770 Healdsburg Ave.
Sebastopol, California 95472
707.823.6331
info@ibisbuilds.com
www.ibisbuilds.com

Ismael Leyva Architects
48 West 37th St.
New York, NY 10018
212.290.1444
212.290.1425 (fax)
ila@ilarch.com
www.ilarch.com

Living Systems Sustainable
Architecture and
Living Systems Building Group
129 Apollo Heights Dr.
Prescott, AZ 86305
928.717.2566
info@michaelfrerking.com
www.michaelfrerking.com

Matson Britton Architects
728 N. Branciforte
Santa Cruz, CA 95062
877.877.3797
info@matsonbritton.com
www.matsonbritton.com

MOBILI, Inc.
Contemporary European Office
and Residential Furniture
P.O. Box 223808
Carmel, CA 93922
831.625.1458
831.625.1481 (fax)
info@mobilig.com
www.mobilig.com

Polshek Partnership Architects, LLP
320 W. 13th St.
New York, NY 10014
212.807.7171
212.807.5917 (fax)
info@polshek.com
www.polshek.com/

Pugh+Scarpa Architects
2525 Michigan Ave., Bldg. F1
Santa Monica, CA 90404
310.828.0226
310.453.9606 (fax)
www.pugh-scarpa.com

Pugh+Scarpa Architects
P.O. Box 6070
Charlotte, NC 28207
704.347.3464
daniel@pugh-scarpa.com
www.pugh-scarpa.com

Rockwell Architecture,
Planning and Design, P.C.
5 Union Square West
New York, NY 10003
212.463.0334
212.463.0335 (fax)
www.rockwellgroup.com

The Sheldrake Organization
132 W 21ST ST
New York, NY 10011
212.242.9353 ext. 149
info@sheldrake.com
www.sheldrake.com

Vince Wucherer Interiors
Santa Cruz, CA
831.331.3184

Photography
Alice Maritz Starek (pages 65–71)
Boulder, CO

Anthony May Photography
(pages 99–105)
4711 N Talmam Ave
Chicago, IL 60625
773.334.7238
info@mayphoto.com
www.mayphoto.com

Barbara Bourne Photography
(pages 34–43)
14 Healdsburg Ave., Ste. D
Healdsburg, CA 95448
707.486.9420
707.433.4499 (fax)
barbara@bbourne.com
www.bbourne.com

Barnes Photographics (pages
12 right, 13, 81–87)
831.338.6623
bphotos@comcast.net
www.barnesphotographics.com

Barry Rustin Photography (pages73–79)
1234 Sherman Ave., Ste. 103
Evanston, IL 60202
847.475.0055
847.475.4065 (fax)
barryrustin@hotmail.com
barryrustinphotography.com

Bruce Fiene (pages 25–33)
Brock Fiono Productions
Worcester, MA

Daniel Nadelbach Photography,
LLC (pages 45–53)
Studio Coyoacan
P.O. Box 3838
Santa Fe, NM 87501
505.982.7004
505.982.7005 (fax)
daniel@nadelbachphoto.com
www.nadelbachphoto.com/

Douglas Johnson (pages 117–125)
3734 Portsmouth Circle
N.Stockton, CA 95219
Tel: 209.952.2100
www.douglasjohnsonphotography.com

Gilda Meyer-Niehof
Makeup& Styling
Studio Coyoacan
Santa Fe, NM 87501
505.982.7004
505.982.7005 (fax)
www.coyoacan.com
www.jadudesign.com

Dave Chengson (pages 89–97)
Aptos, CA

Marvin Rand Photography (pages
5, 9, 11, 12 left, 22–23, 127–135)
1310 Abbot Kinney Blvd
Venice, CA 90291
310.396.3441
310.634.2222 (cell)
marvinrand@ca.rr.com
www.marvinrand.com

Photography by Larry Kantor
(pages 2–3, 137–149)
511 Canyon Springs Rd
Prescott, AZ 86303
928.776.4846
larrykantor@cableone.net
www.photographybylarrykantor.com

Rich Frutchey (pages 15, 16, 18, 19)
Courtesy of Davis Frame Company

Sugar Pine Studios
P.O. Box 1059
Grass Valley, CA 95945
530.477.8732
jim@sugarpinestudios.com
www.sugarpinestudios.com

Wayne Capili: Interface Visual (pages 55–63)
2460 Garden Rd., Ste. D
Monterey, CA 93955
831.372.8830
visual1@mac.com
www.interfacevisual.com

RESOURCES

Recommended Reading
Dave Bonta and Stephen Snyder, *New Green Home Solutions*, Gibbs Smith, Publisher, 2008.
Michael Brower, PhD and Warren Leon PhD, *The Consumer's Guide to Effective Environmental Choices: Practical Advice from the Union of Concerned Scientists*, Three Rivers Press, 1999.
Dan Chiras, *The Homeowner's Guide to Renewable Energy*, New Society Publishers, 2006.
Dan Chiras, *The Natural House: A Complete Guide to Healthy, Energy-Efficient, Environmental Homes*, Chelsea Green Publishing, 2000.
The Editors of E Magazine, *Green Living*, Plume, 2005.
Paul Gipe, *Wind Energy Basics: A Guide to Small and Micro Wind Systems*, Chelsea Green Publishing Company, 1999.
Jeffrey Hollender and Geoff Davis, with Meika Hollender and Reed Doyle, *The Seventh Generation Guide to Safe & Healthy Non-Toxic Cleaning*, New Society Publishers, 2005.
David Johnston and Kim Master, *Green Remodeling: Changing the World One Room at a Time*, New Society Publishers, 2004
James Kachadorian, *The Passive Solar House: Using Solar Design to Heat & Cool Your Home*, Chelsea Green Publishing Company, 1997.
Paula Baker-Laporte, Erica Elliott, John Banta, *EcoNest: Creating Sustainable Sanctuaries of Clay, Straw, and Timber*, Gibbs Smith, Publisher, 2008.
Paula Baker-Laporte, Erica Elliott, John Banta, *Prescriptions for a Healthy House, 3rd Edition: A Practical Guide for Architects, Builders & Homeowners*, New Society Publishers, 2008.
Bill McKibben, *Deep Economy: The Wealth of Communities and the Durable Future*, Times Books, 2007.
Stephen Morris, *The New Village Green*, New Society Publishers, 2007.
Nell Newman with Joseph D'Agnese, *The Newman's Own Organics Guide to the Good Life: Simple Measures that Benefit You and the Place You Live*, Villard Books, 2003.
Greg Pahl, *Natural Home Heating: The Complete Guide to Renewable Energy Options*, Chelsea Green Publishing, 2003.
Greg Pahl, *The Citizen-Powered Energy Handbook: Community Solutions to a Global Crisis*, Chelsea Green Publishing, 2007.
David Pearson, *The New Natural House Book: Creating a Healthy, Harmonious, and Ecologically Sound Home*, Fireside/Simon & Schuster, 1998.
Jennifer Roberts, *Good Green Homes: Creating Better Homes for a Healthier Planet*, Gibbs Smith, Publisher, 2003.
John Schaeffer, *The Real Goods Solar Living Sourcebook*, New Society Publishers, 2005.
Paul Scheckel, *The Home Energy Diet*, New Society Publishers, 2005.
Nancy H. Taylor, *Go Green: How to Build an Earth-Friendly Community*, Gibbs Smith, Publisher, 2008.
Crissy Trask, *It's Easy Being Green,: A Handbook for Earth-Friendly Living*, Gibbs Smith, Publisher, 2006.
Carol Venolia & Kelly Lerner, *Natural Remodeling for the Not-So-Green House: Bringing Your Home Into Harmony with Nature*, Lark Books, 2006.
Alex Wilson, *Your Green Home: A Guide to Planning a Healthy, Environmentally Friendly New Home*, New Society Publishers, 2006.

Sustainable Living Periodicals
BackHome Magazine
P.O. Box 70
Hendersonville, NC 28793
800.992.2546
info@backhomemagazine.com
www.backhomemagazine.com

E Magazine
28 Knight St.
Norwalk, CT 06851
203.854.5559
203.866.0602 (fax)
info@emagazine.com
www.emagazine.com

The Green Guide
The National Geographic Society
1145 – 17th St. NW
Washington, DC 20036
editor@thegreenguide.com
www.thegreenguide.com

Green Living Journal
100 Gilead Brook Rd.
Randolph, VT 05060
802.234.9101
901.234.9101 (fax)
editor@greenlivingjournal.com
www.greenlivingjournal.com

Home Energy Magazine
2124 Kittredge St., #95
Berkeley, CA 94704
510.524.5405
www.homeenergy.org/
contact@homeenergy.org

Home Power
P.O. Box 520
Ashland, OR 97520
800.707.6585
541.512.0343 (fax)
mailbox@homepower.com
www.homepower.com

Mother Earth News
1503 SW 42nd St.
Topeka, KS 66609
800.234.3368
785.274.4305 (fax)
www.motherearthnews.com

Natural Home
1503 SW 42nd St.
Topeka, KS 66609
800.340.5846
www.naturalhomemagazine.com

Sierra
85 Second St., 2nd Fl.
San Francisco, CA 94105
415.977.5500
415.977.5799 (fax)
sierra.magazine@sierraclub.org
www.sierraclub.org

Solar Today
2400 Central Ave., Ste. A
Boulder, CO 80301
303.443.3130
303.443.3212 (fax)
publisher@solartoday.org
www.solartoday.org/

Green Building Associations and Organizations
ACAA—American Coal Ash Association
15200 E. Girard Ave., Ste. 3050
Aurora, CO 80014
720.870.7897
www.acaa-usa.org

American Forest and Paper Association
1111 19th St., NW, Ste. 800
Washington, DC 20036
800.878.8878
www.afandpa.org

American Institute of Architects
1735 New York Ave., NW
Washington, DC 20006
800.242.3837
www.aia.org

APA—The Engineered Wood Association
7011 S. 19th
Tacoma, WA 98466
253.565.6600
www.apawood.org

American Society of Landscape Architects
636 Eye Street, NW
Washington, DC 20001
202.898.2444
www.asla.org

Congress for the New Urbanism
The Marquette Building
140 S. Dearborn St., Ste. 310
Chicago, IL 60603
312.551.7300
www.cnu.org

Consortium for Research on
Renewable Industrial Materials
University of Washington
P.O. Box 352100
Seattle, WA 98195
206.543.0827
www.corrim.org

Energy and Environmental
Building Association
10740 Lyndale Ave. South, Ste. 10W
Bloomington, MN 55420
952.881.1098
www.eeba.org

Environmental Building News
122 Birge St., Suite 30
Brattleboro, VT 05301
802.257.7300
www.BuildingGreen.com

Forest Stewardship Council
1155 – 30th St., NW, Ste. 300
Washington, DC 20007
202.342.0413
www.fscus.org

Global Green USA
2218 Main St., 2nd Fl.
Santa Monica, CA 90405
310.581.2700
www.globalgreen.org
www.treehugger.com

National Associations and Renewable Energy Industry Groups
American Society of Heating, Refrigeration, and Air Conditioning Engineers (ASHRAE)
1791 Tullie Cir., NE
Atlanta, GA 30329
404.636.8400
404.321.5478 (fax)
ashrae@ashrae.org
www.ashrae.org

American Solar Energy Society
2400 Central Ave., Unit G-1
Boulder, CO 80301
303.443.3130
303.443.3212 (fax)
ases@ases.org
www.ases.org/solar

U.S. Department of Energy Office of
Energy Efficiency & Renewable Energy
Energy Efficiency and Renewable Energy
Mail Stop EE-1
Department of Energy
Washington, DC 20585
1.877.337.3463
http://www.eere.energy.gov

Hydronic Radiant Heating Association
123 C St.
Davis, CA 95616
530.753.1100
530.753.4125 (fax)

National Renewable Energy Laboratory
1617 Cole Blvd.
Golden, CO 80401
303.275.3000
303.275.4053 (fax)
webmaster@nrel.gov
www.nrel.gov

Solar Energy Industries Association
805 15th St. NW Suite 510
Washington, D.C. 20005
202.682.0556
info@seia.org
www.seia.org

Sustainable Buildings Industry Council
1331 H St., NW, Ste. 1000
Washington, DC 20005
202.628.7400
202.393.5043 (fax)
sbic@sbicouncil.org
www.sbic.org

National Association of State
Energy Officials (NASEO)
1414 Prince St., Ste. 200
Alexandria, VA 22314
703.299.8800
703.299.6208 (fax)
mnew@naseo.org
www.naseo.org/

National Association of Regulatory
and Utility Commissioners (NARUC)
1101 Vermont, NW, Ste. 200
Washington, DC 20005
202.898.2200
202.898.2213 (fax)
www.naruc.org

Solar Energy Industries Association (SEIA)
1616 H St., NW, Ste. 800
Washington, DC 20006
202.628.7745
202.628.7779 (fax)
www.seia.org

Other Organizations
American Solar Energy Society
2400 Central Ave., Unit G-1
Boulder, CO 80301
303.443.3130
303.443.3212 (fax)
ases@ases.org
www.ases.org

Center for Renewable Energy
& Sustainable Technology
1612 K St., NW, Ste. 202
Washington, DC 20006
202.293.2898
202.293.5857 (fax)
info@crest.org
www.crest.org

National Energy Education
Development Project
8408 Kao Cir.
Manassas, VA 20110
703.257.1117
703.257.0037 (fax)
info@need.org
www.need.org

National Energy Foundation
3676 California Ave., Ste. A117
Salt Lake City, UT 84104
801.908.5800
801.908.5400 (fax)
info@nef1.org
www.nef1.org

National Energy Information Center
U.S. Department of Energy
Energy Information Administration, EI30
1000 Independence Ave., SW
Washington, DC 20585
202.586.8800
infoctr@eia.doe.gov
www.eia.doe.gov

National Renewable Energy Laboratory
1617 Cole Blvd.
Golden, CO 80401
303.275.3000
303.275.4053
webmaster@nrel.gov
www.nrel.gov

N.C. Solar Energy Association
P.O. Box 6465
Raleigh, NC 27628
919.832.7601
ncsea@mindspring.com   www.ncsolar.org

Northeast Sustainable Energy Association
50 Miles St.
Greenfield, MA 01301
413.774.6051
nesea@nesea.org
www.nesea.org

Solar Cookers International
1919 – 21st St., Ste. 101
Sacramento, CA 95814
916.455.4499
916.455.4498 (fax)
info@solarcookers.org
www.solarcooking.org

Solar Energy Industries Association
1616 H St., NW, 8th Fl.
Washington, DC 20006
202.628.7745
202.628.7779 (fax)
info@seia.org
www.seia.org

Solar Now Project
100 Sohier Rd.
Beverly, MA 01915
978.927.9786
978.927.9191 (fax)
solarnow@mediaone.net
www.solarnow.org

Southface Energy Institute
241 Pine St.
Atlanta, GA 30308
404.872.3549
404.872.5009 (fax)
questions@southface.org
www.southface.org

Union of Concerned Scientists
2 Brattle Square
Cambridge, MA 02238
617.547.5552
617.864.9405 (fax)
ucs@ucsusa.org
www.ucsusa.org

University of Central Florida
Regional Service Project III
College of Education, Rm. 146
Orlando, FL 32816
407.823.2950
RSP3@pegasus.cc.ucf.edu

Other Helpful Websites

Environmental Building News
www.buildinggreen.com

Million Solar Roofs Initiative
www.millionsolarroofs.com

National Center for Photovoltaics
www.nrel.gov/ncpv

Renewable Energy Access
www.renewableenergyaccess.
com/rea/home

Renewable Resource Data Center
www.rredc.nrel.gov/

Solar Energy Technologies Program
www.eere.energy.gov/solar

Conservation and Efficiency Resources

Database of State Incentives for
Renewables and Efficiency
www.dsireusa.org

Residential Energy Services
Network (RESNET)
www.natresnet.org

Tax Incentives Assistance Project (TIAP)
www.energytaxincentives.org

Information on proper CFL disposal:
www.lamprecycle.org
www.earth911.org
www.nema.org/lamprecycle/
epafactsheet-cfl.pdf

Residential Energy Services
Network (RESNET)
P.O. Box 4561
Oceanside, CA 92052
760.806.3448
760.806.9449 (fax)
info@natresnet.org
www.natresnet.org

The Energy Conservatory
2801 – 21st Ave., S, Ste. 160
Minneapolis, MN 55407
612.827.1117
612.827.1051 (fax)
info@energyconservatory.com
www.energyconservatory.com

Energy Star
1200 Pennsylvania Ave., NW
Washington, DC 20460
888.STAR.YES
www.energystar.gov/homes

Building America Program
U.S. Department of Energy
www.eere.energy.gov/buildings/
building_america

Passive Heating and Cooling Resources

American Solar Energy Society
2400 Central Ave., Unit G-1
Boulder, CO 80301
303.443.3130
303.443.3212 (fax)
ases@ases.org
www.ases.org

Energy Efficiency and Renewable
Energy Clearinghouse (EREC)
P.O. Box 3048

Merrifield, VA 2216
800.523.2929
703.893.0400 (fax)
doe.erec@nciinc.com
www.eren.doe.gov/consumerinfo

Florida Solar Energy Center
University of Central Florida
1679 Clearlake Rd.
Cocoa, FL 32922
407.638.1000
407.638.1010 (fax)
infor@fsec.ucf.edu
www.fsec.ucf.edu

Home Energy Saver
www.hes.lbl.gov/

National Climatic Data Center
www.ncdc.noaa.gov/oa/ncdc.html

National Association of Home
Builders-Research Foundation
400 Prince George Blvd.
Upper Marlboro, MD 20774
800.638.8556
301.249.3035 (fax)
info@nahb.com
www.nahbrc.org

National Center for Appropriate Technology
P.O. Box 3838
3040 Continental Dr.
Butte, MT 59702
406.494.4572
800.275.6228
406.494.2905 (fax)
info@ncat.org
www.ncat.org

National Renewable Energy
Laboratory (NREL)
1617 Cole Blvd.
Golden, CO 80401
303.275.3000
303.275.4053 (fax)
www.nrel.gov

North Carolina Solar Center
P.O. Box 7401
North Carolina State University
Raleigh, NC 27695
919.515.5666
800.33.NCSUN
919.515.5778 (fax)
ncsun@ncsu.edu
www.ncsc.ncsu.edu/

North Carolina Solar Energy Association
2501 Blue Ridge Rd., Ste. 150
Raleigh, NC 27607
919.832.7601
919.863.4101
ncsea@mindspring.com
www.mindspring.com/~ncsea

Passive Solar Industries Council (PSIC)
1331 H St., NW, Ste. 1000
Washington, DC 20005
202.628.7400
202.393.5043 (fax)
PSICouncil@aol.com
http://www.psic.org/

Solar Thermal Design Assistance Center
Sandia National Laboratories
Mail Stop 0703
Albuquerque, NM 87185
505.844.3077
505.844.7786 (fax)
dfmenic@sandia.gov
www.sandia.gov/Renewable_Energy/
solarthermal/dufdac.html

Southface Energy Institute
241 Pine St.
Atlanta, GA 30308
404.872.3549
404.872.5009 (fax)
info@southface.org
www.southface.org

Sustainable Buildings Industries Council
1331 H St., NW, Ste. 1000
Washington, DC 20005
202.628.7400
202.393.5043 (fax)
sbic@sbicouncil.org
www.sbicouncil.org

Solar Domestic Hot Water Resources
Database of State Incentives for
Renewables and Efficiency (DSIRE)
www.dsireusa.org

U.S. DOE, Office of Energy Efficiency
and Renewable Energy
www.eere.energy.gov/consumer/
your_home/water_heating/
index.cfm/mytopic=12760

Hot Water Savings Tips
www.rredc.nrel.gov/solar/
codes_algs/ PVWATTS

Solar Rating and Certification
Corporation (SRCC)
www.solar-rating.org

Solar Space-Heating Resources
American Society of Heating, Refrigeration,
and Air Conditioning Engineers (ASHRAE)
1791 Tullie Cir., NE
Atlanta, GA 30329
404.636.8400
404.321.5478 (fax)
ashrae@ashrae.org
www.ashrae.org

American Solar Energy Society
2400 Central Ave., Unit G-1
Boulder, CO 80301
303.443.3130
303.443.3212 (fax)
ases@ases.org
www.ases.org/solar

Hydronic Radiant Heating Association
123 C St.
Davis, CA 95616
530.753.1100
530.753.4125 (fax)

National Renewable Energy Laboratory
1617 Cole Blvd.
Golden, CO 80401
303.275.3000
303.275.4053 (fax)
webmaster@nrel.gov
www.nrel.gov

Solar Energy Industries Association
122 C St., NW, 4th Fl.
Washington, DC 20001
202.383.2600
202.383.2670 (fax)
info@seia.org
www.seia.org

Solar Thermal Design Assistance Center
Sandia National Laboratories
Mail Stop 0703
Albuquerque, NM 87185
505.844.3077
505.844.7786 (fax)
dfmenic@sandia.gov
www.sandia.gov/Renewable_Energy/
solarthermal/dufdac.html

Solar Electricity Resources
American Solar Energy Society
2400 Central Ave., Unit G-1
Boulder, CO 80301
303.443.3130
303.443.3212 (fax)
ases@ases.org
www.ases.org

Energy Efficiency and Renewable
Energy Clearinghouse (EREC)
P.O. Box 3048
Merrifield, VA 2216
800.523.2929
703.893.0400 (fax)
doe.erec@nciinc.com
www.eren.doe.gov/consumerinfo

Florida Solar Energy Center
University of Central Florida
1679 Clearlake Rd.
Cocoa, FL 32922
407.638.1000
407.638.1010 (fax)

infor@fsec.ucf.edu
www.fsec.ucf.edu

National Association of Home
Builders-Research Foundation
400 Prince George Blvd.
Upper Marlboro, MD 20774
800.638.8556
301.249.3035 (fax)
info@nahb.com
www.nahbrc.org

National Center for
Appropriate Technology
P.O. Box 3838
3040 Continental Dr.
Butte, MT 59702
406.494.4572
406.494.2905 (fax)
800.275.6228
info@ncat.org
www.ncat.org

National Renewable Energy
Laboratory (NREL)
1617 Cole Blvd.
Golden, CO 80401
303.275.3000
303.275.4053 (fax)
www.nrel.gov

North Carolina Solar Energy Association
2501 Blue Ridge Rd., Ste. 150
Raleigh, NC 27607
919.832.7601
919.863.4101 (fax)
ncsea@mindspring.com
www.mindspring.com/~ncsea

Northeast Sustainable Energy Association
50 Miles St.
Greenfield, MA 01301
413.774.6051
nesea@nesea.org
www.nesea.org

**Financing, Incentive, and
Rebate Resources**
Clean Energy
U.S. Environmental Protection Agency
1200 Pennsylvania Ave., NW (MC 6202J)
Washington, DC 20460
202.343.9442
critchfield.james@epa.gov
www.epa.gov/cleanenergy/

Database of state incentives
for renewable energy
www.dsireusa.org/

Interstate Renewable
Energy Council (IREC)
P.O. Box 1156
Latham, New York 12110
518.458.6059
info@irecusa.org
www.irecusa.org/

Renewable Energy System Design and Installation Resources

North American Board of Certified
Energy Practitioners (NABCEP)
Saratoga Technology & Energy Park
10 Hermes Rd., Ste. 400
Malta, NY 12020
518.899.8186
info@nabcep.org
www.nabcep.org

The Source for Renewable Energy
www.energy.sourceguides.com/index.shtml

Databases of installers:
www.gosolar.com
www.homepower.com/
resources/directory.cfm
www.renewableenergyaccess.com/
rea/market/business/home
www.seia.org/about/statechapters.asp

State Resources
Alabama

Energy, Weatherization, and
Technology Division
Department of Economic
and Community Affairs
401 Adams Ave.
P.O. Box 5690
Montgomery, AL 36103
334.242.5290
334.242.0552 (fax)
www.adeca.state.al.us/EWT/default.aspx

Alabama Solar Energy Center
University of Alabama at Huntsville
Johnson Research Center
Huntsville, AL 35899
800.874.3327 (in Alabama)
256.890.6343
256.890.6848 (fax)

Alaska

Alaska Energy Authority
Alaska Industrial Development
and Export Authority
813 W. Northern Lights Blvd.
Anchorage, AK 99503
907.269.3000
907.269.3044 (fax)
www.aidea.org/aea/index.html

American Samoa

Territorial Energy Office
American Samoa Government
Samoa Energy House, Tauna
Pago Pago, AS 96799
011.684.699.1101
011.684.699.2835 (fax)
www.americansamoa.gov/
departments/offices/energy.htm

Arizona

Arizona Department of Commerce
1700 W. Washington, Ste. 220
Phoenix, AZ 85007
602.771.1201
602.771.1203 (fax)
http://www.azcommerce.com/Energy/

Arkansas

Arkansas Energy Office
Arkansas Department of
Economic Development
One Capitol Mall, Ste. 4B-215
Little Rock, AR 72201
501.682.1370
501.682.2703 (fax)
Energy@1800arkansas.com
www.1800arkansas.com/Energy/

California

California Energy Commission
1516 Ninth St., MS #39
Sacramento, CA 95814
916.654.5403
916.654.4423 (fax)
www.energy.ca.gov

The Real Goods Solar Living Institute
13771 S. Hwy. 101
P.O. Box 836
Hopland, CA 95449
707.744.2017
www.solarliving.org/

Colorado

Governor's Energy Office
225 E. 16th Ave., Ste. 650
Denver, CO 80203
303.866.2100
303.866.2930 (fax)
geo@state.co.us
www.state.co.us/oemc

Connecticut

Energy & Policy Unit, PDPD
Connecticut Office of Policy and
Management
450 Capitol Ave., MS#52ENR
P.O. Box 341441
Hartford, CT 06134
860.418.6416
860.418.6495 (fax)
www.opm.state.ct.us/pdpd2/
energy/enserv.htm

Connecticut Clean Energy Fund
999 West St.
Rocky Hill, CT 06067
www.ctinnovations.com

Delaware

Delaware Energy Office
1203 College Park Dr., Ste. 101
Dover, DE 19904
302.735.3480
302.739.1840 (fax)
www.delaware-energy.com

District of Columbia

D.C. Energy Office
2000 – 14th St., NW, Ste. 300 East
Washington, DC 20009
202.673.6700
202.673.6725 (fax)
www.dceo.dc.gov/dceo/site/default.asp

Florida

Florida Energy Office
Florida Department of
Environmental Protection
3900 Commonwealth Blvd., MS-19
Tallahassee, FL 32399
850.245.8264
850.245.2947 (fax)
www.dep.state.fl.us/energy/default.htm

Florida Solar Energy Center
1679 Clearlake Rd.
Cocoa, FL 32922
407.638.1000
407.638.1010
webmaster@fsec.ucf.edu
www.fsec.ucf.edu

Georgia
Division of Energy Resources
Georgia Environmental Facilities Authority
233 Peachtree St., NE
Harris Tower, Ste. 900
Atlanta, GA 30303
404.584.1000
404.584.1069 (fax)
www.gefa.org/Index.aspx?page=32

Guam
Guam Energy Office
P.O. Box 2950
Agana, GU 96910
671.646.4361
671.649.1215 (fax)
www.guamenergy.com/main/index.
php?pg=contact
www.guamenergy.com/

Hawaii
Strategic Industries Division
Department of Business, Economic
Development and Tourism
235 S. Beretania St., Rm. 502
P.O. Box 2359
Honolulu, HI 96804
808.587.3812
808.586.2536 (fax)
library@dbedt.hawaii.gov
www.hawaii.gov/dbedt/info/energy/

Idaho
Energy Division
Idaho Department of Water Resources
322 E. Front St.
P.O. Box 83720
Boise, ID 83720
208.287.4800
208.287.6700 (fax)
energyspecialist@idwr.idaho.gov
www.idwr.idaho.gov/energy/

Illinois
Energy & Recycling Bureau
Illinois Department of Commerce
and Economic Opportunity
620 E. Adams
Springfield, IL 62701
217.785.3416
217.785.2618 (fax)
www.commerce.state.il.us/dceo/
Bureaus/Energy_Recycling/

Indiana
Office of Energy and Defense
Development
101 W. Ohio St., Ste. 1250
Indianapolis, IN 46204
317.232.8939
317.232.8995 (fax)
www.energy.in.gov

Iowa
Energy & Waste Management Bureau
Iowa Department of Natural Resources
Wallace State Office Building
502 E. 9th St.
Des Moines, IA 50319
515.281.8912
515.281.8895 (fax)
www.iowadnr.com/energy/index.html

Kansas
Kansas Energy Office
Kansas Corporation Commission
1500 SW Arrowhead Rd.
Topeka, KS 66604
785.271.3170
785.271.3268 (fax)
public.affairs@kcc.state.ks.us
www.kcc.ks.gov/energy/

Kentucky
Governor's Office of Energy Policy
Division of Renewable Energy Energy
Efficiency
500 Mero St.

Capital Plaza Tower, 12th Fl.
Frankfort, KY 40601
502.564.7192
504.564.7484 (fax)
marie.anthony@ky.gov
www.energy.ky.gov/default.htm

Louisiana
Technology Assessment Division
Department of Natural Resources
P.O. Box 44156
617 N. Third St.
Baton Rouge, LA 70804
225.342.1399
225.342.1397 (fax)
techasmt@la.gov
www.dnr.louisiana.gov/techasmt

Maine
State Energy Program
Maine Public Utilities Commission
State House Station No. 18
Augusta, ME 04333
207.287.3318
207.287.1039 (fax)
joy.adamson@maine.gov
www.state.maine.gov/msep

Maryland
Maryland Energy Administration
1623 Forest Dr., Ste. 300
Annapolis, MD 21403
410.260.7655
410.974.2250 (fax)
meainfo@energy.state.md.us
www.energy.state.md.us

Massachusetts
Division of Energy Resources
Executive Office of Energy & Environmental
Affairs
100 Cambridge St., Ste. 1020
Boston, MA 02114
617.727.4732
617.727.0030 (fax)
DOER.Energy@state.ma.us
www.mass.gov/doer/

Michigan
Energy Office
Michigan Department of Labor &
Economic Growth
P.O. Box 30221
611 W. Ottawa, 4th Fl.
Lansing, MI 48909
517.241.6228
517.241.6229 (fax)
erdinfo@michigan.gov
www.michigan.gov/energyoffice

Minnesota
State Energy Office
Minnesota Department of Commerce
85 – 7th Pl., E., Ste. 500
St. Paul, MN 55101
651.296.4026
651.297.7891 (fax)
energy.info@state.mn.us
www.commerce.state.mn.us

Mississippi
Energy Division
Mississippi Development Authority
P.O. Box 849
510 George St., Ste. 300
Jackson, MS 39205
601.359.6600
601.359.6642 (fax)
energydiv@mississippi.org
www.mississippi.org/content.
aspx?url=/page/3331&

Missouri
Energy Center
Department of Natural Resources
P.O. Box 176
1101 Riverside Dr.
Jefferson City, MO 65102
573.751.2254
573.751.6860 (fax)
energy@dnr.mo.gov
www.dnr.mo.gov/energy/index.html

Montana
Department of Environmental Quality
P.O. Box 200901
1100 N. Last Chance Gulch, Rm. 401-H
Helena, MT 59620
406.841.5240
406.841.5222 (fax)
www.deq.state.mt.us/energy/

Nebraska
Nebraska State Energy Office
P.O. Box 95085
Lincoln, NE 68509
402.471.2867
402.471.3064 (fax)
energy@neo.ne.gov
www.neo.ne.gov

Nevada
Nevada State Office of Energy
727 Fairview Dr., Ste. F
Carson City, NV 89701
775.687.9700
775.687.9714 (fax)
www.energy.state.nv.us

New Hampshire
Office of Energy and Planning
State of New Hampshire
57 Regional Dr., Ste. 3
Concord, NH 03301
603.271.2155
603.271.2615 (fax)
www.nh.gov/oep/

New Jersey
Office of Clean Energy
New Jersey Board of Public Utilities
44 S. Clinton Ave.
P.O. Box 350
Trenton, NJ 08625
609.777.3300
609.777.3330 (fax)
energy@bpu.state.nj.us
www.bpu.state.nj.us

New Mexico
Energy Conservation and
Management Division
New Mexico Energy, Minerals and
Natural Resources Department
1220 S. St. Francis Dr.
P.O. Box 6429
Santa Fe, NM 87505
505.476.3311
505.476.3322 (fax)
emnrd.ecmd@state.nm.us
www.emnrd.state.nm.us/ecmd/

New York
New York State Energy Research and
Development Authority
17 Columbia Cir.
Albany, NY 12203
518.862.1090
518.862.1091 (fax)
www.nyserda.org

North Carolina
State Energy Office
North Carolina Department of
Administration
1340 Mail Service Center
Raleigh, NC 27699
919.733.2230
919.733.2953
energyinfo@ncmail.net
www.energync.net

North Dakota
Office of Renewable Energy & Energy
Efficiency
North Dakota Department of Commerce
P.O. Box 2057
1600 E. Century Ave., Ste. 2
Bismarck, ND 58502
703.328.5300
701.328.2308 (fax)
dcs@nd.gov
www.ndcommerce.com/

Northern Mariana Islands
Energy Division
Commonwealth of the
Northern Mariana Islands
P.O. Box 500340
Saipan, NMI 96950
670.664.4480
670.664.4483 (fax)
energy@pticom.com
www.net.saipan.com/cftemplates/
executive/index.cfm?pageID=20

Ohio
Office of Energy Efficiency
Ohio Department of Development
77 S. High St., 26th Fl.
P.O. Box 1001
Columbus, OH 43216
614.466.6797
614.466.1864 (fax)
pboone@odod.state.oh.us
www.odod.state.oh.us/cdd/oee/

Oklahoma
Office of Community Development
Oklahoma Department of Commerce
P.O. Box 26980
900 N. Stiles
Oklahoma City, OK 73126
405.815.6552
405.605.2870 (fax)
www.okcommerce.gov

Oregon
Oregon Department of Energy
625 Marion St., NE
Salem, OR 97301
503.378.5489
503.373.7806 (fax)
energy.in.internet@state.or.us
www.oregon.gov/ENERGY/

Pennsylvania
Pennsylvania Bureau of Energy,
Innovations, & Technology Deployment
Department of Environmental Protection
P.O. Box 8772
Harrisburg, PA 17105
717.783.0540
717.783.2703 (fax)
eppaenergy@state.pa.us
www.depweb.state.pa.us/energy

Puerto Rico
Energy Affairs Administration
Puerta de Tierra Station
San Juan, PR 00936
787.999.2200, ext. 2888
787.753.2220 (fax)
mvillanueva@drna.gobierno.pr
www.aae.gobierno.pr/

Rhode Island
Rhode Island Office of Energy Resources
1 Capitol Hill, 2nd Fl.
Providence, RI 02908
401.574.9100
401.574.9125 (fax)
www.riseo.ri.gov

South Carolina
South Carolina Energy Office
1201 Main St., Ste. 430
Columbia, SC 29201
803.737.8030
803.737.9846 (fax)
www.energy.sc.gov/

South Dakota
Energy Management Office
Bureau of Administration
523 E. Capitol Ave.
Pierre, SD 57501
605.773.3899
605.773.5980 (fax)
BOAGeneralInformation@state.sd.us
www.state.sd.us/boa/ose/
OSE_Statewide_Energy.htm

Tennessee
Energy Policy Section
Department of Economic & Community
Development
312 – 8th Ave., N., 10th Fl.
Nashville, TN 37243
615.741.2994
615.741.5070 (fax)
www.state.tn.us/ecd/energy.htm

Texas
State Energy Conservation Office
Texas Comptroller of Public Accounts
111 E. 17th St., 11th Fl.
Austin, TX 78701
512.463.1931
512.475.2569 (fax)
www.seco.cpa.state.tx.us/

Utah
Utah State Energy Program
Utah Geological Survey
1594 W. North Temple, Ste. 3110
P.O. Box 146100
Salt Lake City, UT 84114
801.537.3300
801.538.4795 (fax)
dbeaudoin@utah.gov
www.energy.utah.gov

Vermont
Energy Efficiency Division
Vermont Department of Public Service
112 State St., Drawer 20
Montpelier, VT 05620
802.828.2811
802.828.2342 (fax)
vtdps@psd.state.vt.us
www.publicservice.vermont.gov/
divisions/energy-efficiency.html

Efficiency Vermont
255 S. Champlain St., Ste. 7
Burlington, VT 05401
www.efficiency Vermont.com

Vermont Green Building Network
P.O. Box 5384
Burlington, VT 05402
802.338.7664
info@VGBN.org
www.vgbn.org

Vermont Public Interest Research Group
141 Main St., Ste. 6
Montpelier, VT 05602
802.223.5221
vpirg@vpirg.org
www.vpirg.org

Virginia
Division of Energy
Virginia Department of Mines, Minerals &
Energy
202 N. Ninth St., 8th Fl.
Richmond, VA 23219
804.692.3200
804.692.3238 (fax)
www.dmme.virginia.gov/
divisionenergy.shtml

Virgin Islands
Virgin Islands Energy Office
Department of Planning and Natural
Resources
#45 Mars Hill
Frederiksted, St. Croix, USVI 00840
340.773.1082
340.772.0063 (fax)
dbuchanan@vienergy.org
www.vienergy.org/

Washington
Washington Energy Policy Office
Washington State Office of Trade and
Economic Development
P.O. Box 43173
906 Columbia St., SW
Olympia, WA 98504
360.725.3118
360.586.0049 (fax)
www.cted.wa.gov/portal/alias__cted/
lang__en/tabID__526/DesktopDefault.aspx

West Virginia
Energy Efficiency Office
West Virginia Development Office
State Capitol Complex Bldg. 6, Rm. 645
1900 Kanawha Blvd. E.
Charleston, WV 25305
304.558.2234
304.558.0362 (fax)
www.wvdo.org/community/eep.html

Wisconsin

Wisconsin Office of Energy Independence
17 W. Main St., #429
Madison, WI 53702
608.261.6609
608.261.8427 (fax)
power.wisconsin.gov/

Wyoming

Business & Industry Division—State
Energy Program
Wyoming Business Council
214 W. 15th St.
Cheyenne, WY 82002
307.777.2800
307.777.2837 (fax)
tfuller@wybusiness.org
www.wyomingbusiness.org/
business/energy.aspx

USA Solar Stores

Aesop Solar Store
Rock Hill, SC
803.328.9888
EnergyOptions@AESOPSolar.com
www.AESOPSolar.com

Cavendish Solar Store
1531 Route 131
Cavendish, VT 05142
802.226.7093
cavendish@usasolarstore.com
http://usasolarstore.com

Clear Mountain Solar Store
197 Washington Street
Claremont, NH
603.543.9900
mitch@clearmountainsolar.com
http://www.clearmountainsolar.com

CNE Solar Store
809 Southbridge St. RT 20
Auburn, Ma 01501
508.832.4344
1.877.CNESOLAR
peter@cnesolarstore.com
http://cnesolarstore.com/

Deep Creek Lake Solar Store
37 Towne Centre Way
McHenry, MD 21541
301.387.7171
Stan@DCLsolar.com
http://usasolarstore.com

Earth Advocate Solar Store
6350 VT Route 7A
Sunderland, VT
802.362.2766
earthadv@sover.net
http://www.earthadvocate.com/

Empire Solar Store
6 Brunswick Road
Troy, New York 12180
518.274.4609
empiretroy@usasolarstore.com
http://www.empiresolarstore.com/

Four Winds Solar Store
471 Danbury Road
New Milford, CT
203.517.4606
203.517.4212 (fax)
tvesely@neaenergy.com
http://usasolarstore.com

Green Energy Options
79 Emerald Street
Keene, NH 03431
603.358.3444
GEO@usasolarstore.com
http://usasolarstore.com

USA Solar Store of Gettysburg
2218 York Road (Route 30)
Gettysburg, PA 17325
717.334.5494
gettysburg@usasolarstore.com
http://usasolarstore.com

Greenfield Solar Store
2 Fiske Avenue
Greenfield, MA 01301
413.772.3122
http://usasolarstore.com

Green Works Solar Store
1334 Scott Highway, Route 302
Groton, Vermont 05046
802.584.4977
greenworks@usasolarstore.com
http://usasolarstore.com

Grenergy Solar Store
520 Sheffield Plain Road
Sheffield, MA 01257
413.229.0049
http://usasolarstore.com

Saco Solar Store
Rt. 1, 743 Portland Rd.
Saco, ME 04072
207.283.1413
saco@usasolarstore.com
http://www.sacosolarstore.com

SEA Solar Store
187 New Rochester Road
Dover, NH 03820
603.749.9550
603.749.9551 (fax)
http://www.seasolarstore.com/content/

Skyecrafts Solar Store
8161 State Road 52
Hudson, Florida 34667
727.862.1682
http://www.windandsolarnow.com

SoCal Solar Store
54 North Central Avenue
Upland, CA 91786
909.982.8288
socal@usasolarstore.com
http://usasolarstore.com

Waterbury Solar Store
3487 Waterbury Stowe Road (Rt 100)
Waterbury Center, Vermont
802.244.5600
info@waterburysolar.com